THE GIANT BOOK OF FANTASTIC FACTS

Compiled and ed...
G. Cropper
E. Simpson
A. Burton
P. Hornby

Cover designed by
J. Cooper

Printed in Hungary for the publishers
Peter Haddock Ltd., Bridlington, England

AIR MAIL

The world's greatest balloon postal service operated from the beleagured Paris during the Franco–Prussian War of 1870–71. Balloons were made in the city and carried mail and passengers to unoccupied France. But when the Prussians began shooting the balloons down the service continued only at night.

One night a balloon left bound for Tours, in central France but, during the darkness, the wind changed direction without the two men aboard being aware.

It wasn't until they heard the sound of the sea below them that they realised they weren't going to Tours. They finally landed in a Norwegian snowdrift.

The service carried 3,000,000 letters whilst it operated.

★ ★ ★ ★ ★ ★

One-Eyed Soldiers

Because Mohammed Ali, 19th century ruler of Egypt, discovered that men were deliberately blinding themselves in one eye to avoid service in his army, he rounded them up and two special infantry regiments were formed of the one-eyed dodgers.

Tiny Terrors Ate a Town

One of the world's oldest forms of life is the white ant or termite. Its remains have been found which date back 200,000,000 years. The ability to survive plague, droughts and famine is because they can eat their way through anything.

In Australia, termites chomped their way through half a ton of sheet lead to get at fifteen hundred gallons of beer stored in casks in a cellar. They then drank the lot.

Next they turned their attention to an hotel and ate all the billiard balls.

For years the authorities in Florence, Italy, have been waging a constant war to prevent the city's famous buildings being eaten. Special anti-termite protection, costing £14,000, has been given to the art treasures in the Pitti Palace. In a Sri Lanka prison, termites weakened so much of the brickwork that three prisoners escaped from their cells.

A farmer, digging in his fields near the Egyptian town of Behera, dug up an ancient burial ground. Unfortunately for the town, the cemetery was home to millions of termites. The tiny terrors swarmed into the town, devouring everything in sight, buildings, clothes and food. Within a few weeks the town no longer existed and a new town, away from the termites had to be built to rehouse the homeless population.

Termites have a very highly organised society in their colonies, each member having a particular function to perform. Workers build the "cities" in which they live, huge mounds fifteen or more feet high. They keep the myriad passageways clean and look after the food supplies. Some species keep "herds" of greenflies, feeding them on greenstuff and "milking" the little insects by stroking them so that they exude a honey-like substance.

Soldier termites have special powerful jaws on their large heads, others have sacs of poison which they squirt at enemies. Once a soldier gets a grip on an enemy with his powerful pincers he will never let go, even if his body is torn in two. Some African tribes use this ability to hold cuts together. They will hold the two edges of a cut together and let the soldier termite bite into the flesh, then snap the body off thus providing a primitive but very effective method of stitching.

★ ★ ★ ★

2

Statue to Nothing

In Camden, Maine, USA there stands a 28 ft high statue of one Captain Hanson Gregory. It was erected to commemorate the fact that he invented the hole in the doughnut.

Leader King

When King George II's horse bolted during the early stages of the battle of Deltingen, Bavaria, in 1743, the King took his place at the head of his troops on foot, the last British king to do so.

POSTED - A BANK !

In 1916, when the governors of the bank at Vernal, Utah, USA decided the community needed a modern, brick-built bank they came up against a snag.

The nearest brick suppliers were at Salt Lake City 407 miles away. As Vernal had no railway freight carriers were quoting £2 a hundredweight to haul the bricks needed to build the 70 ft by 97 ft building, total cost of transport would be a prohibitive £2,000. But they discovered that the bricks could be sent by post at less than half that.

Postal regulations stipulated the weight of a package should not exceed 50 lb so packages of 10 bricks at a time began to flow through the postal system.

It wasn't long before a postal inspector came to find out what the delay was in other packages. He found the local man with mounds of bricks to deliver to the Vernal bank.

At this they limited the consignments to 200 lb a day but the directors got round this by getting local farmers and townfolk to become consignees for the bricks.

Noble Ancestors

THE HUGE SHIRE HORSES OF TODAY ARE DESCENDED FROM THE WARHORSES OF THE MEDIEVAL KNIGHTS – SPECIALLY BRED TO CARRY THE ENORMOUS WEIGHT OF ARMOUR WORN IN THOSE DAYS. *THE ANIMAL ITSELF WEIGHED ALMOST A TON.*

Handy Creatures

Using tools is not only a human accomplishment, lots of creatures of all species adopt things around them for use. One bird uses a thorn to dig out grubs from rotten wood whilst the aptly named Butcher Bird spikes mice and voles on a thorn bush, providing a larder for when he needs a snack. Seagulls are fond of clams but the shells are too hard for the seagull's beak so it carries the clams over rocks and drops them to crack open the shell.

In the Indian Ocean is a species of crab with a soft shell, so to protect itself it will hold a sea anemone in each claw and uses them to attack its enemies.

Make a Note of it . . .

The method of the fox in delousing itself is probably typical of the crafty animal. It collects wool from the hedges where sheep have passed and, holding the wool in its mouth, slowly submerges itself in a stream until the wool is just on the surface. It then releases the wool which floats downstream. When this wool has been examined it has been found to be full of fleas. As the fox submerges the fleas swarm up to the only dry place − the wool!

You've probably heard the expression "working like a beaver" and this is well borne out by the animal's industry. Using teeth and feet, they build dams of trees, stones and mud which are extremely strong. Dams of more than 1,000 ft in length are not uncommon and one in Montana is 2,100 ft long.

The Sexton Beetle performs a useful service to itself and nature by burying any dead mice or birds it finds. A pair will excavate the soil beneath the corpse until it sinks into the earth. The body is covered and the beetle lays its eggs near it to provide a good supply of food when the little beetles hatch.

A type of wasp digs a hole in sandy ground in which it deposits its eggs, next it kills insects and puts them with eggs to provide a ready supply of food when the young hatch. To protect its eggs from predators the wasp holds a pebble in its mandibles to push sand into the hole and smooth the surface over.

Getting the Bird

The terrifically high cost of installing a telephone in Majorca was given the bird by the residents of the resort of La Rapita so, to order supplies from the nearest town 14 miles away, they started a daily pigeon post. Within half-an-hour of the order being received the goods are on the way by road.

In Russia the keen eyesight of the pigeons is put to a very practical use, at one factory in Moscow they are used to sort ball-bearings.

After four or five weeks special training, the birds inspect the ball-bearings as they pass on a conveyor, if any show the least blemish the pigeons peck a special plate which operates a reject sign, the faulty bearing is removed and the bird rewarded with a few millet seeds.

The Russians claim the pigeons are so expert they can even detect a fingerprint on a bearing and can inspect 4,000 an hour.

But, sire, it does claim to remove all signs of grey hair

Bald Facts

When Louis XIV, one of the vainest men in history, lost all his hair, he vowed no one would ever see his bald head, except his personal barber. Even he was only allowed to see the royal pate very occasionally when he freshened it up with scented water. Each morning he had to hurry along to the King's bedroom and pass the fine, golden, curly wig through the curtains of the royal four-poster bed. Late each night he had to collect it.

Ah, well, Mary, hair today gone tomorrow

Like Elizabeth, Mary Queen of Scots, became bald. After eighteen years imprisoned in England, her death warrant was signed by Elizabeth and, as the axe fell on her neck, her secret was revealed as the executioner held up the severed head, her wig came off exposing her bald head.

7o wigs and she has to wear green with a red dress.

Elizabeth the First lost all her hair by the time she reached middle age and after that she never looked in a mirror again, in fact, she had mirrors banned in the Court.

Elizabeth owned over seventy different wigs of various colours, one was made of bright green silk. Like Louis XIV no one was allowed to ever see her bald except her own personal maid.

Years later, Marie Antoinette, wife of Louis XVI, lost her hair shortly after her marriage and took to wearing elaborate wigs. But, during the French Revolution, her wig was taken away from her when she was imprisoned and her captors made much fun of her baldness but she was allowed to keep a white cap on which was removed on the guillotine, to the derisive laughter of the mob.

FAVOURITE SUBJECT

ARTIST ANTHONY VAN DYCK (1599-1641) PAINTED KING CHARLES THE FIRST'S PORTRAIT NO FEWER THAN 36 TIMES.

MONUMENT ~TO A LEFT LEG!

IN NEW YORK STATE, U.S.A. IS A MONUMENT TO A LEFT LEG. IT WAS ERECTED TO SYMBOLIZE A WOUND RECEIVED BY BENEDICT ARNOLD IN THE WAR OF INDEPENDENCE. HE WAS A HERO THEN BUT LATER HE WENT OVER TO THE BRITISH SIDE.

BUBBLE AND POP

STEAM AND GASES RISING FROM THE SURFACE OF A LAKE IN JAVA CONDENSE INTO GIANT BUBBLES 6 FEET IN DIAMETER.

AFTER FLOATING HIGH INTO THE AIR THEY EXPLODE WITH A LOUD POP

13 - LUCKY FOR HIM.

RICHARD WAGNER, FAMOUS GERMAN COMPOSER, CONSIDERED 13 TO BE HIS LUCKY NUMBER. HE WAS BORN IN 1813 HAD 13 LETTERS IN HIS NAME, HE LEFT SCHOOL AT 13, WROTE 13 OPERAS, LOVED 13 WOMEN IN HIS LIFE. HIS YEAR OF BIRTH ADDS UP TO 13 AND HE DIED ON FEBRUARY 13th. 1883.

PULLING THE PLUG MADE CANAL DISAPPEAR

In 1978 a gang of workmen were given the job of dredging a section of the Chesterfield—Stockwith canal, removing old prams, rusty bedsteads, etc. Amongst the assorted rubbish they dredged up was a huge chain which they attached to a winch and hauled aboard their boat.

Knocking off for a lunch break, the chain was left safely stowed aboard the dredger.

However, on returning to their vessel, they found it sitting on the canal bed and a policeman, who had been investigating a giant whirlpool in the canal, standing on the bank

On a closer inspection of the chain it was found that a 200-year-old plug was attached to it — they had pulled the plug and drained a 1½ mile stretch of water!

All the records had been destroyed in a fire during the war and the plug forgotten about.

Fly Swat War

Algeria became French territory because, during a heated argument between Algerian ruler, Bey Hussein, and the French Consul, Bey Hussein lost his temper and hit the Consul on the head with a fly-swatter. War was declared between the two countries and, in 1830, Algeria was conquered.

☆ ☆ ☆ ☆ ☆ ☆ ☆ ☆

Hitting High Notes

Elizabeth Billington, English opera singer of the 18th century, was renowned for her powerful voice but it nearly got her lynched in Naples, Italy, in 1704. During one of her performances the volcano Vesuvius picked that time to erupt. The scared Italians blamed it on her singing.

MONEY TO BURN

When the professor of Fine Art at the Munich Academy heard about the paintings of Max Raffler he visited the old man in the Bavarian village of Greifenberg and was most impressed, Max was a natural primitive painter.

Max, who lived with his two sisters Maria and Fanny, began painting as a child after an illness had left him mentally backward. He loved painting and painted every day, putting the finished pictures on the top of his wardrobe. The professor, Roth, sent some of the paintings to an international exhibition in Amsterdam, where they were immediately hailed as brilliant, none sold for less than £1,000.

When professor Roth asked what had happened to all the other works, he found that Maria and Fanny, as the pile on the wardrobe got higher, had burned them to make more room — some £25,000,000 worth, over the years!

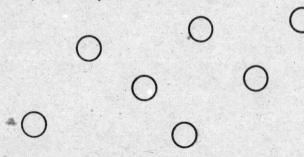

Mixed-up Milker

In 1890, a cow called Mollie, from Ohio, USA began giving black milk. The phenomenon had the scientists of the day baffled. But the milk tasted very good as did the butter made from it, although it did look like a slab of coal tar.

You been at the blackberries again?

GEORGE WASHINGTON (1732-1799)

FIRST PRESIDENT OF THE U.S.A. WAS ALSO ITS FIRST MILLIONAIRE. HE DIED IN THE LAST HOUR OF THE DAY, THE LAST DAY OF THE WEEK, OF THE LAST MONTH OF THE YEAR OF THE LAST YEAR OF THE CENTURY.

SIGNALMAN BABOON

TOWARDS THE END OF THE LAST CENTURY A BABOON IN PRETORIA, SOUTH AFRICA, WORKED AS A SIGNALMAN. NOT ONLY WAS HE ABLE TO WORK THE SIGNALS BUT DID THE HOUSEKEEPING, FETCHED WATER AND OTHER RAILWAY DUTIES. HE ALSO USED TO PUSH HIS LEGLESS HUMAN COMPANION ABOUT ON A TROLLEY. SADLY JACK, FOR THAT WAS HIS NAME, WAS KILLED BY A TRAIN WHILST COLLECTING TITBITS OFF THE LINE THROWN TO HIM BY PASSENGERS.

WELCOME STRANGER

A NUGGET OF GOLD WEIGHING 2,280¼ TROY OUNCES WAS PICKED UP IN A CART RUT IN VICTORIA, AUSTRALIA IN 1869.

IT WAS NAMED THE 'WELCOME STRANGER'

BABY KING

HENRY VI SUCCEEDED TO THE THRONES OF ENGLAND AND FRANCE AT THE AGE OF NINE MONTHS, AUGUST 31, 1422.

SPORT FOR THOUGHT

Ten Day Match

The longest cricket match of all time was the Test between England and South Africa in Durban. It was played from 3rd to the 14th March, 1939. After ten days, the game had to be stopped because the English team's boat was leaving for home!

? ? ? ? ? ?

"Kid Climber"

Only ½ hour after he is born a mountain goat can stand quite firmly and indeed will most probably try to climb up the nearest hill.

? ? ? ? ? ?

How Long Does It Take You To Solve a Rubik Cube?

It took Minh Thai just 22.95 seconds on 5th June, 1982, in the World Rubik Cube Championship in Budapest.

Who Was the Heaviest Goalkeeper?

He was 6 feet 3 inches tall, when he played for Bradford City he weighed 26 stones, he was an England International, he once stopped a game by snapping the crossbar in two. Who was he?

His name was Willie J. "Fatty" Foulke (1916–1974)

124 Miles On Ice

Each year in the Netherlands there is an ice-skating race called the "Tour Of The Eleven Towns". It originally began in the 18th century and the journey takes in 124 miles of rivers, lakes and canals, town after town.

26 Miles On Land?

Do you know how many miles make a marathon and why it is so called?

It stems from ancient Greek when a soldier had to run with a special message from Sparta to a town called Marathon, a distance of just under 26 miles.

When the Olympic Games were revived in 1896 the so called "marathon" was adopted from that particular run, setting a new distance of 26 miles, 385 yards.

Bowled Over!

Did you know there are 65,000,000 bowlers in the world — there is an Alley in Japan which has over 500 lanes!

The sport is thought to have originated in Egypt when children used large stones set up as pins and used small stones as a ball.

0—40 mph!

A baby ostrich can run as fast as his parents — that is 40 mph — fast enough to escape from most hunters. And did you know that a kick from an adult ostrich is so powerful that it could break your leg!

SPORT FOR THOUGHT

On Yer Bike!

An American, Thomas Stevens, was the first person to ride around the world on a bicycle. It took him 3 years to complete the trip.

Tee Off!

The ancient Romans first played a game like golf using bent wooden sticks and a leather ball stuffed with feathers. Then, in the Middle Ages, the Dutch played a similar game on ice using a wooden club to hit a stake in the ice.

In 1457 James IV banned the game in Scotland for he feared his soldiers would not devote enough time to practice their archery skills.

What is the Most Popular Game in the World?

Why, Soccer of course. It is a very easy game to learn, can be played almost anywhere and all you need is a ball.

It is played by over 140 nations throughout the world and draws the most spectators.

There is one bird which can fly all day long without even flapping its wings — an albatross.

The only horse to win the Grand National three times was Red Rum. He won in 1973, 1974 and 1977. He was second in 1975 and 1976.

The Biggest Jumper

Fleas can jump up to 10 inches high — many, many times their own height.

In the 1600s, Queen Christine of Sweden, detested fleas so much she ordered a miniature canon to be built — it was only 4 inches long — she fired it whenever she saw a flea, but it is not known whether or not she was successful in killing any.

Some Swimmer

Amazing isn't it — but yes, Elephants can and do swim — top speed — guess what, 2 miles per hour! They can't jump though!

Did you know that when a sea urchin walks — it walks on the tips of its teeth!

Shortest Boxing Match

The shortest boxing match lasted just 10½ seconds
in 1946 between R. Walton and A. Coutoure.

Who's the Strongest Then?

It is astonishing to learn that an Ant can lift much
more weight than Man. Average Man can lift a little
more than his own weight, whereas on Ant can lift 50
times his own weight.

The First Messenger

A well trained homing pigeon has been recorded to
travel home over strange land for no less than 1,500
miles — thousands of years ago Man bred and used
pigeons just for carrying messages.

Killer Tiger

In India a tigress was shot in 1911 — her crime? —
she had killed over 400 people in just 8 years before
being caught.

COCK-EYED HILL

The farmer driving his horse and cart to Moncton, New Brunswick, Canada, in 1802, stopped on a gently sloping hill to fix a loose shoe on his horse. After unhitching the animal he placed a rock behind a cart wheel to prevent it rolling back down the slope.

It did that alright, what it didn't do was to stop the cart rolling UPHILL!

The strange story of the upside-down hill soon spread and people came for miles around to test the hill for themselves with balls or carts.

Today a modern road covers the old track and a sign erected by the authorities, tells motorists to switch off their engines and enjoy a ride uphill.

Nobody can say why this phenomenon exists.

★　★　★　★

Bear Fruits

The Polar bear is a giant, weighing up to 1,000 lbs. Its natural food is the seal, it can scent food up to 10 miles away and has been seen swimming at a steady 4 or 5 miles an hour, over 100 miles from the nearest land.

Eskimos call the bear Nahnook and they pressed the Canadian government to outlaw the white hunters, even though the hunters have to pay the Eskimos £1,000 for every bear they kill.

Over the past few years 5,000 of the animals have been shot in Northern Canada and 3,000 in Norway. Russia banned the killing of Polar bears in 1965.

The Fattest Man Ever!

The fattest man who ever lived weighed 1,069 pounds when at his greatest weight. Incredibly, this is more than half a ton. At this time his waist measured 122 inches.

He was Robert Earl Hughes who was born in 1926 in Illinois, USA. At birth he weighed 11½ pounds but by the time he was six years old his weight had risen to over 200 pounds, and when he was 18, it was almost 700 pounds.

Hughes toured with a carnival during the last years of his life, and it was whilst he was touring in Indiana in 1958 that he became ill. He had to be treated in his caravan parked outside the hospital as he was too fat to get through the hospital door.

He died soon afterwards and his coffin was made from a piano case. A crane had to be used to lower the coffin into the ground because it was so heavy.

TOMB OF ICE

As the whaling schooner "Hope" was passing a huge ice barrier in the Southern Ocean, on September 22, 1860, the ice parted to reveal a ship encrusted with ice, its sails hanging in shreds. Captain Brighton, of the "Hope" boarded the craft and found the perfectly preserved corpse of the captain of the ship "Jenny" seated, with pen in hand, before an open log book. The last entry read "May 4th, 1823, no food for 71 days. I am the only one alive." Seven crew members, a woman and a dog were all that were found aboard.

ARE YOU SURE THAT THE SUN IS STILL THERE?

TRAVELLING AT THE SPEED OF 186,325 MILES PER SECOND IT TAKES THE LIGHT OF THE SUN 8½ MINUTES TO REACH THE EARTH ~ IT IS ALSO ESTIMATED THAT THE SUN LOSES WEIGHT AT THE RATE OF 1,000,000 TONS A SECOND!

A REAL FOUR-EYES –

LIU CH'ING WAS BORN WITH TWO PUPILS IN EACH EYE! BUT THIS DOUBLE DEAL OF NATURE DIDN'T STOP HIM FROM ENTERING PUBLIC SERVICE AND, IN A.D. 955, HE BECAME THE GOVERNOR OF SHANSI PROVINCE

STINKING BLOOM

THE RAFFLESIA ARNOLDI, OF SUMATRA, IS THE LARGEST BLOSSOM IN THE WORLD MEASURING 3 FEET ACROSS – IT ALSO GIVES OFF AN OVERPOWERING STENCH OF ROTTING CARRION.

– AND A THREE-EYE

THE **TUATARA** LIZARD, OF NEW ZEALAND, STILL GROWS THE RUDIMENTS OF A THIRD EYE ON THE TOP OF ITS' HEAD –

– A LINK WITH THE TIME WHEN THE CREATURE HAD MANY FLYING ENEMIES.

PICKPOCKET QUEEN

Little Jenny Webb arrived in the seething London of 1721, from a country orphanage where she was born 14 years before. She was the illegitimate child of a maidservant and an aristocrat. Jenny got a job mending clothes but really she was learning to become a thief. She was a good learner and by the time she was 18 she was the head of a gang of 40 pickpockets.

She would frequent churches wearing a pair of false arms, with her own arms concealed beneath her dress. Slits in the sides of the dress enabled her to "relieve" the surrounding worshippers of their bags and purses.

But she was eventually caught and sentenced to transportation for life to the American colonies, but soon bribed her way back to England.

However, she was caught again and this time, sentenced to death. Thousands turned up at Tyburn gallows, and her band of thieves did a roaring trade selling broadsheets of her life story. So died England's Queen thief at the age of 34.

Summing it up

"Mirror image" addition — with the same answer

```
1 2 3, 4 5 6, 7 8 9          9 8 7, 6 5 4, 3 2 1
1 2 3, 4 5 6, 7 8              8 7 6 5 4 3 2 1
1 2 3, 4 5 6, 7                 7 6 5 4 3 2 1
1 2 3, 4 5 6                     6 5 4 3 2 1
1 2 3, 4 5                        5 4 3 2 1
1 2 3, 4                           4 3 2 1
1 2 3                               3 2 1
1 2                                  2 1
1                                     1
```
_____   _____
```
1, 0 8 3, 6 7 6, 2 6 9       1, 0 8 3, 6 7 6, 2 6 9
```
_____   _____

Even if you don't like figures, multiplying 12345679 by 99999999 is simple

```
              × 1 2 3 4 5 6 7 9
                9 9 9 9 9 9 9 9
              _____
                1 1 1 1 1 1 1 1 1
               1 1 1 1 1 1 1 1 1
              1 1 1 1 1 1 1 1 1
             1 1 1 1 1 1 1 1 1
            1 1 1 1 1 1 1 1 1
           1 1 1 1 1 1 1 1 1
          1 1 1 1 1 1 1 1 1
         1 1 1 1 1 1 1 1 1
        1 1 1 1 1 1 1 1 1
        _____
        1 2 3 4 5 6 7 8 9 8 7 6 5 4 3 2 1
        _____
```

Have you ever noticed that in the nine times table all the answers add up to nine? Here is an example, check the others yourself.

$$1 \times 9 = 9$$
$$2 \times 9 = 18 \quad (1 + 8 = 9)$$
$$3 \times 9 = 27 \quad (2 + 7 = 9)$$
$$4 \times 9 = 36 \quad (3 + 6 = 9)$$
$$5 \times 9 = 45 \quad (4 + 5 = 9)$$

and so on

More peculiarities of number nine appear below

$$9 \times 9 + 7 = 88$$
$$98 \times 9 + 6 = 888$$
$$987 \times 9 + 5 = 8888$$
$$9876 \times 9 + 4 = 88888$$
$$98765 \times 9 + 3 = 888888$$
$$987654 \times 9 + 2 = 8888888$$
$$9876543 \times 9 + 1 = 88888888$$
$$98765432 \times 9 + 0 = 888888888$$

Amazing, isn't it? But there's more

$$65359477124183 \times 17 \times 1 = 1111111111111111$$
$$65359477124183 \times 17 \times 2 = 2222222222222222$$
$$65359477124183 \times 17 \times 3 = 3333333333333333$$
$$65359477124183 \times 17 \times 4 = 4444444444444444$$
$$65359477124183 \times 17 \times 5 = 5555555555555555$$
$$65359477124183 \times 17 \times 6 = 6666666666666666$$
$$65359477124183 \times 17 \times 7 = 7777777777777777$$
$$65359477124183 \times 17 \times 8 = 8888888888888888$$
$$65359477124183 \times 17 \times 9 = 9999999999999999$$

Sky Walking Braves

In 1886 The Dominion Bridge Company had the tricky problem of bridging the St Lawrence River at Montreal. It was a perilous job and there were so many accidents the chief engineer feared he would soon lose all his best steel riggers. He was amazed one day to see dozens of spectators standing casually on the steel girders high above the swirling river. They were Mohawk Indians and showed no fear at all of the height at which they stood, some were even carrying small children.

Here was the solution to the engineer's problem of manpower. So the Mohawks began their career as steeplejacks.

Since then they have formed the hard core of America's skyscraper builders. They take a pride in erecting the paleface's buildings. One Indian, well named Thomas Sky, said "The pay isn't so much when you think of how much our employers will make out of the property when its finished. And they don't risk their lives."

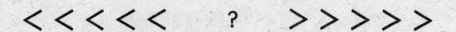

What is the Oldest Industry in the World?

Many people would think that farming is the oldest industry — in fact, the oldest industry is the production of chopping tools and axes, known as "flint knapping" which started about 1,750,000 years ago.

Dark Horse

Towards the end of the Second World War, Bill Smith arrived in Queensland, Australia, with two racehorses and applied for a licence to be a jockey and a trainer. Other jockeys were always puzzled as to why Bill Smith never changed into his racing silks when they were present — that is until "he" died aged about 80 Then the secret was revealed, Bill Smith was a woman whose real name was Wilhelmina.

Women were not allowed to race at that time so, posing as a man, she rode in many races over a 30 year period — Australia's first female jockey, even though no one knew it at the time.

Our Democratic World

The largest election in the world was the Election for the Indian "House of the People". It had 529 seats and 362,000,000 voters.

Did you know that if you live in the Philippines, you can vote at the age of 15? You have to wait a little longer in Andorra, until you are 25!

The whole of North Korea turned out to vote in the election of 1962 — and they all voted for the same party — the Worker's Party of Korea!

One of the virtues supposedly attributed to an MP is honesty. However, one man who didn't possess this quality was President Charles King of Liberia, who in 1927 claimed a majority over his rival of 234,000 — the "majority" was more than 15½ times larger than the population of his country eligible to vote!

Did You Know . . .

. . . that there are three people who have camped out since March, 1974? They have slept outside in temperatures sometimes of around minus 67°F, minus 55°C. They are Sven and Per (brothers) and their sister Kari Heistad of Lebanon, New Hampshire in America. In extreme temperatures they can use up to three sleeping bags!

27

FREEFALL MARCH 23. 1944.

FLIGHT SJT. ALKEMADE, FACED WITH BURNING TO DEATH IN A BLAZING R.A.F. BOMBER OVER ENEMY TERRITORY, DECIDED TO JUMP -AT 18,000 FT. WITHOUT A PARACHUTE! BUT AMAZINGLY HE LANDED WITHOUT SERIOUS INJURY IN A FOUR FOOT DEEP SNOWDRIFT. THE OFFICER IN CHARGE OF THE GERMAN SEARCH PARTY TESTIFIED THAT ALKEMADE HAD NO PARACHUTE HARNESS ON NOR WAS THERE ANY SIGN OF A PARACHUTE.

THE OCTOPUS IS A REAL QUICK-CHANGE ARTIST. IT IS ABLE TO CHANGE RAPIDLY FROM A DULL CRIMSON THROUGH A ZEBRA PATTERN TO A DULL GREY. IT CAN MATCH ITS SURROUNDINGS IN A FEW SECONDS.

ALTHOUGH THE **THE GREAT FIRE OF LONDON** (1666) DESTROYED THOUSANDS OF DWELLINGS PLUS CHURCHES, HOSPITALS, WAREHOUSES ETC. ONLY SIX PEOPLE LOST THEIR LIVES. ONE GOOD THING ABOUT THE FIRE IS THAT IT HELPED TO CHECK THE PLAGUE WHICH WAS RIFE IN LONDON AT THE TIME.

Where is the World's Largest Pyramid

One normally associates pyramids with ancient Egypt, but surprisingly, the world's largest pyramid is in Mexico. It is called the Quetzalcoatl and was built around the year 100 of sun dried bricks and earth. Although only 177 feet high, it covers an area of 45 acres.

The tallest pyramid, however, is the Pyramid of Cheops in Egypt, which was originally 480 feet high. It covers an area of 13 acres.

It has been estimated that the Mexican pyramid is a million cubic yards greater in volume than the Pyramid of Cheops.

The Wilstar Group Holding Co, set up by William Stern in 1971, was declared bankrupt for £104,390,248 in February, 1979. He applied to the Appeal Court in March 1982 to be discharged on an offer to pay £55,000 over 3 years. His application was rejected by the Court as "impudent".

Who Was the First To Cross the Arctic?

The British Trans-Arctic Expedition whose team consisted of the leader, Wally Herbert, Allan Gill, Dr. Roy Koerner and Major Ken Hedges. On their journey, the temperatures dropped to minus 47°F, minus 43.8°C, it was the longest journey on polar ice and needed 40 huskies to help them. The journey started at Barrow Point in Alaska on 21st February 1968 and ended 464 days later on 29th May, 1969 at the Seven Island Archipelago, north east of Spitzbergen. They covered a total of 2,920 miles, which is more than the 1662 miles between the two points. This was because of a drift of 700 miles.

The Crossing of the Antarctic

Dr Vivian Ernest Fuchs led a team of twelve who started their trek on 24th November, 1957 and crossed the pole, they travelled 2,158 miles in 99 days from their starting point of Shackleton Base to their finishing point of Scott Base, crossing the South Pole between the two points.

What is the Commonest Name for a Pub?

The answer is "The Red Lion", there are more than 5,000 in Britain.

The Amazing Case of David

David, when a young boy, seemed to be mature and knowledgeable far beyond his years, he not only began to show knowledge of this time but of life many centuries ago.

When he was seven he went with his father to visit Naples in Italy. They became friendly with an archaeologist who invited them to see a recently-excavated Roman villa on the fringe of the city.

When they arrived at the site, David became excited and started running about the place stopping only when he found a Roman bath decorated with polished blue tiles. On the tiles were the signs of the Zodiac.

David shouted, "Here's our bath and our tiles — mine had a bull on it and the fish was Marcus's." As soon as the little lad said that name he burst into tears and begged his father to take him away.

On another occasion they were visiting some caves on the island of Guernsey, which had once housed French prisoners. Suddenly, the youngster went to the cave wall and tapped on it saying that there was another cave beyond and a man had been walled-up in it. He said he had watched the walling-up and even gave the name of the man.

The Guernsey authorities finally agreed to investigate although they knew nothing of another cave.

But, sure enough, a door was found which had been bricked-up — and inside was the skeleton of a man.

A subsequent search in the records proved that the boy was right about the man's name.

One other time, David and his brother were on a visit to the British Museum. Looking at some Egyptian mummies, David remarked that there should be some special marks on the underside of one of the cases. When his father asked him to draw these marks, he drew three Egyptian birds, explaining, "That was my name, but you weren't there then, I was a kind of inspector and I had to mark the coffins if they were satisfactory."

So, how could David have known about the three birds, the secret cave, and the tiles? Was his present life the fourth time on earth, or one in many? Maybe reincarnation is the explanation.

CURSE OF THE

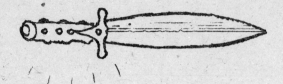

It sounds as if the story of the Herero knife, its gold handle studded with jewels, had come from the pen of a fiction writer, but not so. The knife carried a curse — at least 28 people suffered a violent death after coming into contact with it.

The story of the knife begins back in 1917 when it came into the possession of a German army officer, Lieutenant Froelich. He believed that the chief of the African Herero tribe knew the whereabouts of a treasure trove. Froelich and three soldiers kidnapped the chief and his wife and tortured the woman with the knife until the chief was forced to tell that the fortune in gold was buried in a certain kraal. The lieutenant led his three soldiers against the kraal and slaughtered everyone in it. The officer then murdered two of his own men, his mind filled with greed.

But other natives had seen the massacre and followed Froelich and his companion as they drove off in a wagon loaded with treasure. While they slept that night, the two Germans were killed and their bodies left with the wagon — and the treasure.

Twenty-five years passed and two gold prospectors chanced to camp on the spot. The sands had buried the treasure wagon and the two men, searching for firewood came across the top of the wagon.

Mainly out of curiosity, the two men scooped away the sand and uncovered the two skeletons of Froelich and his companion and the gold — plus the tarnished knife.

The two men polished the knife up and took off into town to sell the gold, this done, they bought tickets for Johannesburg the next day. But that night one of the men was killed in a drunken brawl.

The other man sold the knife to a firm of jewellers in Johannesburg, Cohen and Rosenblatt.

Cohen took the knife to show to his wife, a few hours later the couple were killed by burglars who broke into the house.

Already 25 people had died after being connected with the knife but Cohen's son, to whom the dagger had passed, scoffed at the idea that it carried a curse. Some weeks later, while driving his new sports car, he spun off a straight road and crashed over a cliff. He was number 26. From now on no one wanted to own the dagger and it passed quickly from hand to hand.

One man, named Sturman, bought and displayed it on the wall of his home. A few days later he was killed by lightning.

The knife lay unclaimed amongst Sturman's effects until a wealthy American instructed his agent in Africa, Dark Nathan, to purchase it for him. Nathan bought it and quickly hurried to dispatch it at the Post Office relieved to get rid of the accursed blade. As he walked out of the Post Office, Nathan was run down and killed by a lorry.

From that time nothing more has been heard of the Herero dagger. With such a reputation no one wishes to find it.

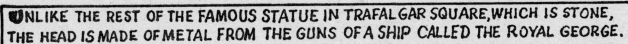
UNLIKE THE REST OF THE FAMOUS STATUE IN TRAFALGAR SQUARE, WHICH IS STONE, THE HEAD IS MADE OF METAL FROM THE GUNS OF A SHIP CALLED THE ROYAL GEORGE.

TIPPING THE TOPPER

IN OLDEN TIMES, NOBLEMEN WHO WERE TO BE EXECUTED, WERE EXPECTED TO TIP THE AXEMAN FROM 7 TO 10 POUNDS 'FOR HIS SERVICES'

IT'S A BLOOMING RARITY

THE GIANT PUYA PLANT OF MEXICO BLOOMS ONLY ONCE IN ITS 150 YEARS OF LIFE — AND THEN DIES! HUNDREDS OF LITTLE FLOWERS APPEAR IN THE LAST FEW DAYS OF ITS LIFE WHEN THE PLANT GROWS TO A HEIGHT OF 20 FEET.

WHAT IS WRONG WITH THIS PICTURE?

THE PENGUINS—THEY ARE FOUND ONLY SOUTH OF THE EQUATOR.

The first playing cards were invented about 600 years ago, but no-one knows who the inventor was.

The symbols of each suit stand for the different social classes of the 14th century, while the picture cards represent various historical figures. The first packs produced contained 78 cards but that many proved too difficult to handle. The Joker was the super trump card and was the only one of the old pack to survive when the number was trimmed down.

IT'S ON THE CARDS

DIAMONDS represent the wealthy classes.
SPADES represent soldiers. The word "spade" comes from the Spanish word for sword, which is "spada".
HEARTS represent churchmen, the symbol used to be a chalice, a communion cup, but the shape was gradually modified to the familiar heart-shape.
CLUBS are the poorer people and the symbol represents the cudgels carried by this class.

The King of Diamonds is Julius Caesar and his wife is Rachel, for whom Jacob toiled for 7 years.
The King of Spades is David, slayer of Goliath. His card Queen is the Greek Goddess of War, Pallas, who carries both a sword and a flower. The Knave is the Danish Hogier, cousin of Charlemagne.
The King of Hearts was based on the mighty Charlemagne, he conquered half of Europe around 800 AD. As a special tribute to his military greatness, he is the only King to brandish his sword. His card Queen is Judith, the Biblical heroine. She slew an Assyrian general with his own sword.

Lastly, the King of Clubs goes way back in history and is Alexander the Great, conqueror of most of the known world in 323 BC. In early designs, he was shown with a world globe in his hand, this was later shown as an orb on his coat.

The Queen of Clubs is the only Englishwoman in the pack, no less than Queen Elizabeth I. Her Knave is one of the Knights of the Round Table, Sir Lancelot.

Impossible Accidents

Scholastic experts have always said that the Bible story of Jonah and the whale was an impossibility, a whale just isn't capable of swallowing a man. But it has happened. In February 1891, the crew of American whaler, Star of the East, were attempting to harpoon a large sperm whale from two boats. The animal thrashed about and overturned one of the boats, two sailors disappeared. When the whale was eventually captured and cut up, one of the men, James Bartley, was found, still alive, in the whale's stomach. Bartley, describing his experience, said, "The whale threw me into the air, I found myself in a slippery channel, then a sort of large sack. I lost consciousness."

A tragic, freak accident happened when Bavarian sculptor, Daniel Hagar, was putting the finishing touches to a group of figures he had worked on for years. Unfortunately, his hammer struck off a 4 inch marble splinter which penetrated his heart, killing him instantly.

Charles Croucher was killed by wearing too tight a collar. Croucher, a motor attendant, was found slumped by the wall of a pumping station where he was employed at Portsmouth. At the inquest the doctor said the man had apparently been drinking, and was asphyxiated by his own tight collar.

In a lighter vein, Sid Wicks, boxing Alf Blandford at London's Stadium Club, thought he was a sure loser when his opponent was about to deliver a terrific right swing. But Alf missed, over-balanced and fell, striking his jaw on the floor. The impact knocked him cold.

An elderly Danish man, who had dismounted to adjust his bicycle chain, tried to stand up but was painfully jerked back to his knees, he had caught his beard in the chain. He had to remain in this position until a man with a sharp knife came along and cut him free. Thereafter he became clean shaven.

KNOW YOUR BODY?

Did you know there are 206 bones in you body? The femur is the biggest, the smallest is in your middle ear.

Can you match this — there once was a man in India who grew his finger nails to the incredible total length of 116½ inches.

Colourblindness

Males are more prone to colourblindness than females, in fact 1 in 200 females suffer against 1 in 12 men.

Usually a sufferer cannot distinguish between such colours as yellow and light green. Some people are fully colourblind — all colours appear in shades of black and white.

Did you know that messages transmitted by your nervous system can travel as fast as 180 mph?

How Much Do You Think Your Brain Weighs?

Females weigh approximately 2 lbs 12 oz and males 3 lbs 2 oz and both getting heavier!

KNOW YOUR BODY

In — Pulses?

A healthy person's pulse beats at the rate of 75 per minute — smaller animals need a higher rate because they lose more heat through their bodies. Amazing isn't it — a small bird has a pulse rate of 200 beats per minute, an elephant has only 25!

When You're Tired

The more you move your muscles, the more they produce a fluid called "sarcolactic acid" which gathers around the muscle, making it "tired".

When you sleep or rest, your body rids itself of this acid, repairs your joints and re-charges your nerve cells.

Are You Any Wiser With Your Wisdom Teeth?

Is there any truth in the saying that when you get your wisdom teeth, you are wiser?

No — it is just an assumption that, hopefully, as you are older — you will be wiser.

Are You One In a Million?

You need an IQ of 180 or over to be that!

$$\frac{1}{1,000,000}$$

Calorie Count

Calories are a measure of food energy. It depends on how old you are as to how many you need. For instance, a 65 year old lady only needs about 1600 calories per day — the same as needed by a 4 year old. Also, in a warm climate you need less and in a cold climate many more calories are needed.

What have a lady aged 25 years and a man aged 65 in common? Almost equal muscular strength!

KNOW YOUR BODY?

Sweet Dreams

Did you know that we all dream every night — some of us remember them and some don't. And we move about 40 times in our sleep. Poor sleepers as much as 70 times.

?

A Spoonful of Sugar Keeps the "Hiccups" Down

Yes, it's true. It has been proved that it can work on some people.

?

Did you know that there is a man who started hiccups in 1922 and hasn't stopped yet!

What grows faster during the day than it does at night? What grows faster during the summer than winter? Have you guessed yet? Why, the answer is your Hair — it can grow as much as 9 inches in one year.

Why Do We Suffer From Seasickness?

Believe it or not, but it begins in your ears — not your tummy.

Your sense of balance is controlled by canals in your ears filled with "lymph". When the ship rocks, the motion causes the lymph to move around which eventually sends signals to the brain. This disturbance to the nervous system results in dizziness and sickness.

Skin Deep

Do you realise that if the skin of an adult was peeled off and placed flat on the ground, it would cover an area of over 18 square feet!

What consists of 91% water? Plasma (blood).

KNOW YOUR BODY?

You Give Me Fever!

The highest body temperature record where the patient survived was 112°F. Normal temperature is 98.°F.

When you are ill, your body fights the sickness by working harder, producing more blood cells, your lungs breathe faster, helping your body to rid itself of wastes and poisons whilst fighting the disease. With this "burning up" process, your temperature rises — hence a "fever".

Frostbites

In cold weather, your toes or fingers may become so cold that blood stops circulating around them. When the blood stops, so does oxygen and without oxygen, cells begin to die.

If frostbite is neglected, it can lead to gangrene, the death of tissues due to lack of oxygen, hence you must consult with your doctor in serious cases.

Treatment: apply warmth very gently to the area.

Yawning — Is It Contagious?

Yes it is, in fact, I bet you might have yawned already whilst reading this. When your body is tired, your respiratory system slows down and a spasm in the muscles of your throat takes place, forcing you to take in more air — hence a yawn!

Vitamin "Sea"

In the 19th Century, an English doctor discovered that if you ate lemons or limes, it helped prevent scurvy. From then on, all English sailors had a ration of lime juice — hence the nickname "limey".

PRICE OF CANADA -
ONE PENNY

SIR WILLIAM ALEXANDER, THE EARL OF STIRLING (1567-1640) RECEIVED A GRANT FROM JAMES THE FIRST OF ALL THE LANDS OF CANADA, NOVA SCOTIA, ALL THE BAYS, RIVERS, ISLANDS, MINES AND FORESTS. THE PRICE ~ ONE SCOTTISH PENNY PAYABLE ON CHRISTMAS DAY.

YET THE EARL DIED INSOLVENT HAVING SPENT A FORTUNE IN AN ATTEMPT TO DEVELOP HIS VAST ESTATE.

THE BRACHIOSAURUS,
WHICH ROAMED THE EARTH SOME 150,000,000 YEARS AGO, WAS 75 FT. LONG, WEIGHED 40 TONS AND YET HAD A BRAIN WHICH WEIGHED ONLY **7 OUNCES**.

SEA UNICORN
THE NARWHAL, A SMALL ARCTIC WHALE, GROWS A SPIRAL IVORY TUSK WHICH CAN ATTAIN A LENGTH OF **9 FEET**.

Special Language Used by the Mahouts

The men who are the elephant keepers of India, use a language to control the animals which is over 1,500 years old. The oldest in the world still in use.

≪ ≪ ≪ ≪ ≪ ◯ ≫ ≫ ≫ ≫ ≫

HOT RECEPTION

Marauding Vikings, attacking the province of Friesland, on the North Sea, put the male defenders to rout — but the womenfolk had different ideas — they drove off the invaders by pouring scalding hot porridge over them.

The event was incorporated into the Freisian coat of arms which still features an iron porridge pot over **1,000** years later.

Beware of the Bed

Are you a thrasher-about in bed? Well, best fit a safety belt. According to a West German insurance company's statistics, some 600 people a year die in that country by falling out of bed.

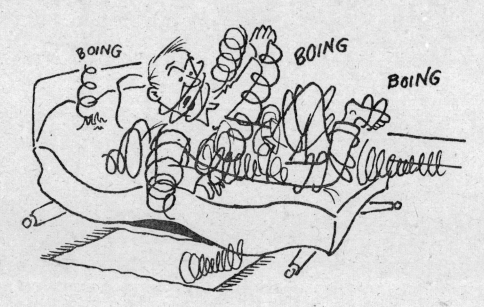

Several years ago, a Sheffield man had a nightmare experience when his bed collapsed and he became imprisoned in a mass of tangled bedsprings; the more he struggled, the worse his situation became. It was five days before neighbours, puzzled by his absence, investigated and freed him, luckily, little the worse for his experience.

A man in California, sleeping on one of those collapsible beds that convert into a settee, was rather restless. This caused the mechanism to slip during the night and the bed closed on its hinges, leaving only his head visible. His friend, who shared the apartment, was unable to free him. Firemen eventually freed him.

A broken mattress spring caused a Scotswoman some pain, but not in her neck. The local doctor had to give pain-killing injections until she was released.

In August 1960, a Middlesex woman was talking so loudly in her sleep that she woke herself up, then found she had dislocated her jaw in her sleep. Similarly, two days earlier, a Cheshire man was taken into hospital after having dislocated his shoulder turning over in bed.

Even sportsmen are at risk in bed. In 1966, six-footer Joachim Ziesche was sleeping in a bed too small for him. Twisting and turning to get comfortable, he wrenched his ankle and put himself out of the ice hockey championships in Yugoslavia.

So be warned, watch out for that bed, it could be dangerous!

The Moonless Month

The month of February 1866, was in one way the most remarkable in the world's history. It had no full moon. January had two full moons as did March, but February had none. According to astronomers, the phenomonen will not occur again for another 2½ million years, so I shouldn't hang about waiting for it.

Day of Rest?

Every day of the week is Sabbath for someone, somewhere.

Sunday it's the Christian Sabbath, Monday it's the Greeks, Tuesday for the Persians, Wednesday for the Assyrians, Thursday for the Egyptians, Friday for the Mohammedans and Saturday for the Jews.

DEAD LEADER

CID CAMPEADOR, RUY DIAS (c1040-99) FAMOUS SPANISH MILITARY HERO, KNOWN AS **EL CID**, LED HIS ARMY INTO BATTLE - AFTER HIS DEATH! HIS EMBALMED BODY WAS SECURED IN THE SADDLE OF HIS WAR HORSE AND, AT THE HEAD OF HIS FOLLOWERS, ADVANCED TO DO BATTLE WITH THE MOORS UNDER KING BUCAR - AND WON A GREAT VICTORY.

E

IS THE MOST USED LETTER IN THE ENGLISH LANGUAGE.

BATTLING CEASAR (161-192)

COMMODUS LUCIUS AELIUS AURELIUS EMPEROR OF ROME, FOUGHT AND WON 1,031 BATTLES IN THE GLADIATORIAL ARENA, A WRESTLER, NARCISSUS, FINALLY STRANGLED HIM TO DEATH.

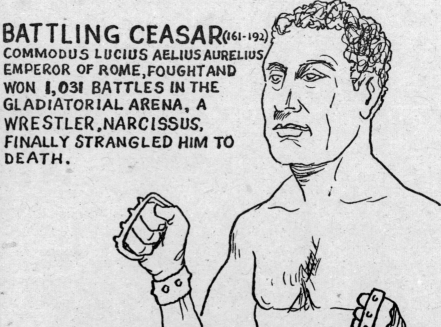

Famous Composers

Probably the most prolific composer of modern times was Frenchman Darius Milhaud who, by the age of 68, had written more than 300 works, including symphonies and ballets.

Probably the most prolific composer of all time was Mozart (1756–1791). He died at the young age of 35, yet he produced over 600 works, symphonies, concertos, operas and numerous orchestral and instrumental works. He wrote his opera "Mithridites" at the age of 4! It was acclaimed an immediate success.

☆ ☆ ☆ ☆ ☆ ☆ ☆ ☆ ☆ ☆ ☆

Imperfect Carpets

No pattern on an Oriental carpet is perfect, a deliberate mistake is always made, for to be perfect it would be challenging Allah, the only one who is perfect.

A carpet, now in the Victoria and Albert Museum, was entirely hand-made by one man, Maksoud, for the mosque in the holy city of Ardebil.

He started work on it when he was 25, and the job took him 40 years. It is 34 feet long and contains 380 hand-tied knots to the square inch — a total of 33,038,200 knots.

Animals in Court

It was not uncommon in the Middle Ages for animals to be tried in courts of law. These prosecutions were based on the Biblical law of Moses which stated that, "If an ox gore a man or woman that they die, then the ox shall be stoned and his flesh shall not be eaten".

Horses, rats, pigs and even insects have been taken to court on various occasions. In 1445, at St Julien, an action was taken against some beetles which had ravaged a vineyard. The insects declined to attend court, so the case fizzled out.

In the 16th century, a clothes moth was put on trial in Spain, charged with destroying a valuable tapestry. The moth was found guilty and sentenced to have its throat cut — actually, it was innocent, it was the larvae who were the real culprits.

In France in 1314, a bull was hanged for goring a man and in 1457, a sow and her six young piglets were sentenced to death for eating a child. The sow was executed, but the piglets got off on account of their youth.

Bird Brain

During the American Civil War a Confederate General by the name of Ewell frequently had hallucinations when he believed he was a bird. During these times he would chirp like a bird and eat nothing but wheat grains.

CHIRP CHIRP

DREAM FORTUNE

John Chapman, tired and hungry, trudged wearily along the dusty road to London. The tinker, from Swaffham in Norfolk, was on his way to London because of a vivid recurring dream. It had been a long hard road and what little money he'd had had been spent, but the dream had been so real he was determined to reach London Bridge for the dream had told him he would meet a man there who would make him rich.

At long last he reached his destination, looking intently at the faces of the thronging strangers. All day he searched but no one spoke to him except to tell him to get out of the way. Towards the end of the day, bitterly disappointed, he cursed himself for being such a fool and turned to make his way home. But, at that moment, a well dressed man approached him. "What is your business here, friend?" he asked, "I have been watching you and I am rather curious."

The tinker looked at him warily, "Why sir, I am here merely on account of a dream I had."

"A dream?" the man said, "that's strange, I myself had a dream about a place I know not and a person I know not, I would have thought myself a fool if I had taken notice of it."

Chapman pressed him to tell of it.

"I was told to go to a place called Swaffham and dig beneath the one tree in the garden of a man called Chapman, and there I would find a crock of gold," the stranger continued.

John Chapman gasped in amazement and he was about to tell of his dream, but his native caution checked him and he agreed it was indeed a foolish dream.

After that John Chapman could hardly get home fast enough, his weariness was forgotten and at last he reached home. Although tired out by his journey he hurried into his garden with a spade and began to dig beneath the solitary tree.

Soon there was a clink as his spade struck an earthenware pot. It was brimful with gold coins! His hardship over the past few days had been well worthwhile. Then, he saw on the lid of the pot, an inscription which read, "Under me doth lie one richer than I."

True enough, after more digging, he found another pot larger than the first and also filled with gold.

His dreams had been proved true.

Far fetched it may seem, but in 1485 a north aisle was added to Swaffham Church. John Chapman, tinker, provided the money. In the same building is a prayer-desk with a carving of John Chapman, his wife and dog.

HANGED-3 TIMES!

CAPTAIN KIDD THE PIRATE, EXECUTED AT WAPPING, LONDON, IN 1701, WAS HANGED THREE TIMES - BECAUSE THE ROPE SNAPPED TWICE. EACH TIME THE ROPE BROKE THE CROWD OF SPECTATORS URGED KIDD TO RUN FOR IT BUT THE PIRATE WAS TOO DRUNK EVEN TO STAND PROPERLY.

MINI MOUSE

THE RARE ETRUSCAN MOUSE OF ITALY, VERY FEW HAVE EVER BEEN CAUGHT, WEIGHS IN AT AROUND ONE TENTH OF AN OUNCE YET IT WILL FEARLESSLY ATTACK ANOTHER ANIMAL TWICE ITS SIZE. IT HAS TO EAT ALL THE TIME, DEVOURING DOUBLE ITS OWN BODY WEIGHT EACH DAY.

IT'S A LIE!

YOUNG GEORGE WASHINGTON NEVER DID CHOP THAT CHERRY TREE DOWN. THE STORY WAS INSERTED INTO THE "LIFE OF WASHINGTON" BY MASON WEEMS WHO USED IT TO EXEMPLIFY THE "TRIUMPH OF TRUTH". WEEMS WAS NOTORIOUS FOR HIS FABRICATIONS.

Safe as the Bank

As safe as the Bank of England today. But on one occasion it wasn't.

One day in 1836, the officials of the bank, received a letter from a man saying that he had found a way he could enter the bullion room any time he pleased.

As the letter was anonymous it was ignored as a hoax. So he wrote again, suggesting a "break-in test" naming a date and time.

They couldn't ignore it this time, so at the appointed time, officials and police locked themselves in the room amongst the stacks of gold ingots. Sure enough, at the appointed time, noises were heard underfoot, a floorboard was removed and a man emerged.

The officials were astounded as the man, James de Maid, a sewer repairman, explained how he had discovered an old disused tunnel which ran close beneath the bullion room.

Only his sense of honesty prevented a fortune from literally "going down the drain". The grateful officials rewarded him with £800 and plugged the leak.

When the Earth Quakes

The biggest-ever recorded earthquake happened in 742 and totally destroyed 300 towns in Egypt, Palestine and Syria.

In 1662, an earthquake centred on Peking in China, buried 300,000 people in the ruins.

Two centuries later, the same area shook again and 100,000 people died.

Another 'quake in China started in 1333 and continued for 10 years.

All Saints Day 1756 saw one of the greatest earthquakes in comparitively recent times when 50,000 people were buried in the ruins of Lisbon. Shocks were felt in Germany, Sweden, Britain and even as far as Canada. The huge tidal wave which the shock created reached the shores of America and swamped several West Indies islands. 700,000 square miles of dry land and ocean bed were affected and sailors far out at sea were thrown from the decks of their ships by the shock.

On the Irish coast, the waves rose breaking over jetties and dashing boats to pieces in the harbours.

At Cadiz the sea level rose an amazing 64 feet!

GHOST SHIP OF THE ARCTIC

Mystery still surrounds the 1,300 ton supply ship Baychimo, owned by the Hudson's Bay Company.

It was abandoned in October 1931, after being trapped in the Arctic ice of Alaska. For about two days it was blowing hard and visibility was limited. About midday it cleared for a while and the crew on the ice saw that the ship had gone from where it had been anchored.

No search could be made until the blizzard had ended. When it finally blew itself out, no trace of the ship could be found.

The Baychimo was sighted a week later by a trapper. It was on top of pack-ice near Point Barrow, 60 miles away. Captain John Cornwell and his crew boarded the vessel and unloaded part of the cargo of furs and took them to a nearby Eskimo village.

When they returned to get the rest of the cargo the ship had disappeared again.

Nothing more was heard of the Baychimo until 1933 when it was sighted hundreds of miles from its original position. A year later it was boarded by Norwegian sailors close to the spot where it was first abandoned.

Since then it has been sighted over 50 times still drifting about the Arctic. On March 11, 1962, fishermen reported having seen the wandering ship in the Beaufort Sea, north of Alaska. Where is it now? It could still be drifting about or sitting on the sea bed, nobody knows for sure.

? ?

Do you suffer from TRISKAIDEKAPHOBIA?

It's a plague that affects all Europe but it only means fear of the number 13.

Go to any street in a French town and you won't find a house numbered 13, the Italians leave it out of lotteries. All over Britain, superstitious people fail to turn up for work on the 13th of the month. One Scotsman spends every Friday the 13th in his bed and won't eat anything for fear of food poisoning or choking.

When Geneva's new international airport was built in 1968, number 12 departure and arrival channels were followed by number 14. Even on the 24 hour clock, 1pm doesn't appear as 13 hours but as 12a. An airport spokesman said, "The majority of passengers are definitely superstitious".

When the Rolling Stones found that they were to fly to America on January 13th 1967, only Mick Jagger took his seat, the others followed later.

The origin of the reputation of 13 is probably linked with the number of people at the Last Supper, and Friday the 13th, the unluckiest of all dates because the crucifixion took place on Friday.

American businessman, Nick Matsoukas, said it was ridiculous, people still don't close business deals on the 13th. They refuse to make decisions. They find reasons to stay at home. He reckoned triskaidekaphobia costs America £100,000,000 a year. Nick wasn't bothered by number 13 — he was the thirteenth of 13 children and had 13 letters in his name. He even organised an anti-superstition demonstration in Athens on February 13th with 13 girls who were to smash mirrors, throw away lucky horseshoes and rabbits feet.

Alas, the demonstration was postponed, Mr Matsoukas had a heart attack two days before.

51

WOLVES OF THE SEA

KILLER WHALES, HUNTING IN PACKS, WILL ATTACK ANYTHING THAT SWIMS IN THE SEA EVEN THE BIGGER WHALES, TEARING AT THEM WITH THEIR SHARP TEETH. SEALS, DOLPHINS AND EVEN PORPOISES ARE SWALLOWED WHOLE.
IN THE STOMACH OF ONE OF THESE KILLERS OVER A DOZEN SEALS AND PORPOISES WERE FOUND.

CHAMPION PILL POPPER

SAM JESSUP OF LINCOLNSHIRE, ADDICTED TO PILL SWALLOWING, TOOK IN THE REGION OF 227,000 IN 22 YEARS. HE ALSO DRANK 40,000 BOTTLES OF MEDICINE. HE DIED IN 1752

BUSYBODY

Mrs. THERESA VAUGHN, 24, APPEARED IN COURT AT SHEFFIELD, 1922 ON A CHARGE OF BIGAMY, CONFESSED TO 61 BIGAMOUS MARRIAGES WITHIN THE SPACE OF 5 YEARS. HER 'HUSBANDS' WERE SCATTERED ALL OVER BRITAIN, GERMANY AND EVEN SOUTH AFRICA.

HENRY FORD,

THE MOTOR MILLIONAIRE, NEVER THREW AWAY A LETTER OR A BILL AND HIS LAWYERS WERE LEFT TO SORT OUT 5,000,000 DOCUMENTS - A TWO YEAR TASK.
AMONGST THEM WERE 10,000 UNOPENED LETTERS.

SOCIALIST PIRATE

The most unusual socialist state ever was founded by French pirate Misson. He had amassed so much booty by 1674 that he decided to retire. On the advice of a friend, a renegade priest named Caraccioli, he chose Madagascar as the ideal place.

With his pirate crew, Misson built a fortified town on the island and called it Diego Suarez, the whole area he named Libertatia, and guaranteed freedom and civil rights to any pirate or deserting seaman.

Libertatia was the world's most unusual socialist state, everything was shared out to all equally, money, food and goods, all the proceeds of the pirates activities.

Misson gave himself the title of Lord Conservator, Caraccioli became Secretary of State, and an American pirate, Thomas Tew, Admiral of the Pirate Fleet.

A new language was invented, no-one could own property, but each man could have as many wives as he wished, including women taken from attacks on Dutch and Portuguese ships. Most of the heavy work was done by Africans freed by the pirates from slave ships.

In 1694, the Portuguese, angered by the pirate's attacks on their merchant ships, sent a force of warships to destroy the Misson fleet and town. The mission was a failure.

But, a year later, the natives, upset by the number of their women leaving to "marry" the pirates, formed a force and attacked the landward side of the town which was unfortified.

The Lord Conservator Misson managed to escape, but his ship sank in a storm. Secretary of State Caraccioli died fighting. Tew died later in a battle with Indian pirates. So ended the state of Libertatia, the few pirates who were left went native, and today there are many light-skinned natives on the island — descendants of the citizens of Libertatia.

Tomb of Proof

Ben Wangford, a naval officer, did not believe in life after death, and to prove it he asked to be buried with a fig in his hand when he died. If it didn't grow he would be right, if it did grow he would be wrong. The tomb, in Watford Parish churchyard, was burst open by the fig tree.

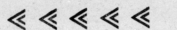 

The year was 1943, half the world was at war and ships were prime targets for German U-Boats. One such victim was the Ben Lomond, a British merchantman, steaming 750 miles off the mid-Atlantic Azores, when it was torpedoed.

Poon Lim, a steward on the ship, took to a life-raft and his ordeal began. He had neither oars nor sail and only emergency rations on the raft.

Drifting at the mercy of the Atlantic, the tiny raft was, at times, becalmed for days, at other times, it was tossed about by winter gales. It was 133 days later and almost 2,000 miles away from where the ship sank that Poon Lim was spotted by some Brazilian fishermen and taken on board their boat.

No solitary shipwrecked sailor has ever survived so long. Poon Lim had lost quite a deal of weight, 3 stones, but was unharmed. On the personal recommendation of Winston Churchill, he was awarded the British Empire Medal in recognition of his courage.

54

All For Art

J. M. W. Turner, wanting to see exactly what a snowstorm at sea was like, had himself lashed to the mast of a Harwich steamer, there he stayed for a freezing four hours. But he produced a painting which is now in the National Gallery. Famous artist, Leonardo da Vinci needed to see a real look of fear — so he pretended to set himself on fire to scare his housekeeper — and painted the expression of horror on her face.

When German artist Philip Hackert was painting his version of the Russian victory over the Turks at Tschesme in 1770, he was unable to imagine what a ship looked like when being blow up. So, anything to oblige, Prince Orloff sent a ship to where the artist was working in Leghorn, Italy, and had it blown to bits for the benefit of Hackert.

On the gruesome side, Giovanni Bellini, 15th century Italian artist, was painting the scene of Salome carrying the head of John the Baptist but couldn't quite get the right effect. The Sultan of Turkey, who had commissioned the picture, had a slave beheaded in front of the artist. The horrified Bellini fled back to Venice.

Talking Room

The word "parlour" originated in monasteries where one room was set aside in which the monks were allowed to speak (parler).

The word "parliament" also comes from the same root, and we all know what a lot of talking goes on there.

FLY SPY

RICHEBOURG, A FRENCHMAN, WAS THE SMALLEST OF DWARFS TO REACH MATURE YEARS, DYING AT THE AGE OF 90 IN 1858. DURING THE FRENCH REVOLUTION RICHEBOURG, WHO WAS ONLY 1 FT. 11 INS. HIGH, CARRIED DESPATCHES IN AND OUT OF PARIS DISGUISED AS A BABY IN THE ARMS OF A NURSEMAID.

HOT SPOT

A FIRE, BELIEVED TO HAVE BEEN STARTED BY A CARELESS HUNTER, HAS BEEN BURNING ON NOVAYA SIBIR ISLAND IN SIBERIA SINCE 1951. THE FIRE IS FED BY COAL NEAR TO THE SURFACE.

ABSENT QUEEN

CHRISTIANE EBERHARDINE, QUEEN OF POLAND 1697-1727, NEVER SET FOOT IN THAT COUNTRY DURING THE WHOLE OF HER 30 YEARS REIGN.

COLD SPOT

IT IS SO COLD IN VERKHOYANSK, SIBERIA, THAT BOILING WATER POURED FROM A KETTLE WOULD BE SOLID ICE WHEN IT REACHED THE GROUND.

For Convenience

Franz Mendl, of Vienna, Austria, moved into a new home and was intrigued as to why his lavatory door was all of 3 inches thick. He began to wonder what could be so valuable in the small room to warrant such protection. So he systematically stripped the room but found nothing.

Later his wife was vacuuming when she accidentally bumped the door with the cleaner and heard it rattle. Swinging the door to and fro she head the rattle again.

Franz examined the door and found it was hollow. When he cut into it he found a bag with uncut diamonds in. They turned out to be worth £28,000.

Another man, Fred Rice, of North London, lifted a loose floorboard in his loo. He was amazed to find a wallet and cash-box underneath. His late father had hidden them there because he didn't trust banks, they contained £1,400 in cash.

Moving from the smallest room to the living room, a man in Stockholm, Sweden, was stripping old wallpaper in preparation to re-decorating when he found an old envelope bearing an 1880 stamp. It proved to be a rarity and was auctioned for the nice, tidy sum of £20,000.

WILLIAM THE CONQUEROR

KILLED TWO MEN AFTER HE DIED!

HE MET HIS DEATH AT ROUEN IN 1087, WHEN HE WAS OUT RIDING. HIS HORSE REARED AND HIS SADDLE POMMEL WAS FORCED INTO HIS STOMACH CAUSING FATAL INTERNAL INJURIES. HIS BODY WAS LAID OUT AND EMBALMERS SENT FOR. THE TWO UNFORTUNATES WHO CAME TO DO THE JOB CAUGHT A FEVER FROM THE CORPSE AND BOTH DIED WITHIN A FEW DAYS.

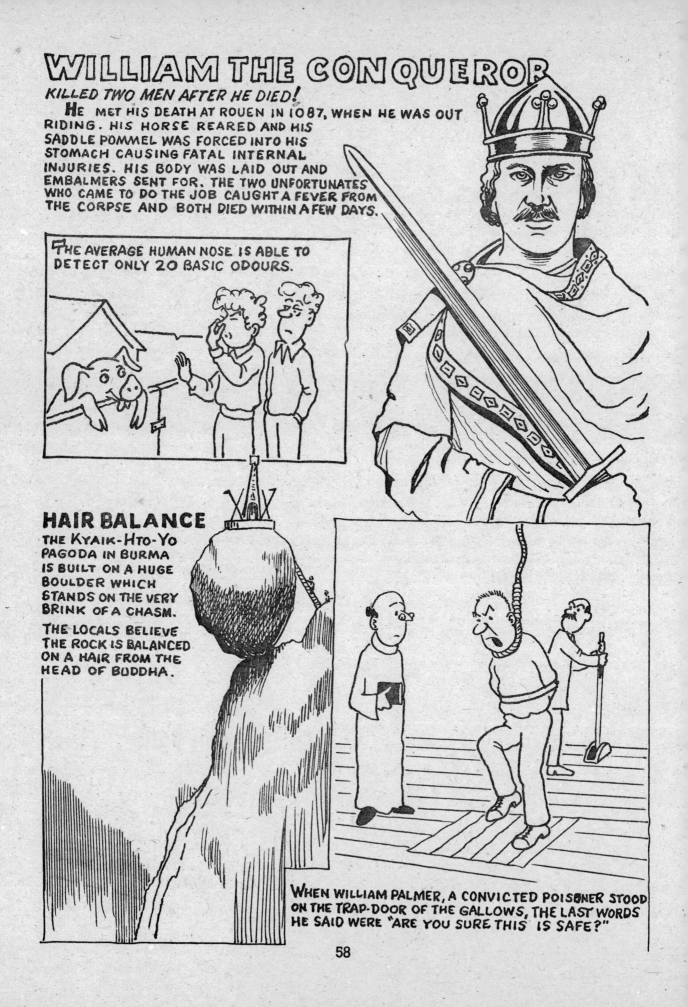

THE AVERAGE HUMAN NOSE IS ABLE TO DETECT ONLY 20 BASIC ODOURS.

HAIR BALANCE

THE KYAIK-HTO-YO PAGODA IN BURMA IS BUILT ON A HUGE BOULDER WHICH STANDS ON THE VERY BRINK OF A CHASM.

THE LOCALS BELIEVE THE ROCK IS BALANCED ON A HAIR FROM THE HEAD OF BUDDHA.

WHEN WILLIAM PALMER, A CONVICTED POISONER STOOD ON THE TRAP-DOOR OF THE GALLOWS, THE LAST WORDS HE SAID WERE "ARE YOU SURE THIS IS SAFE?"

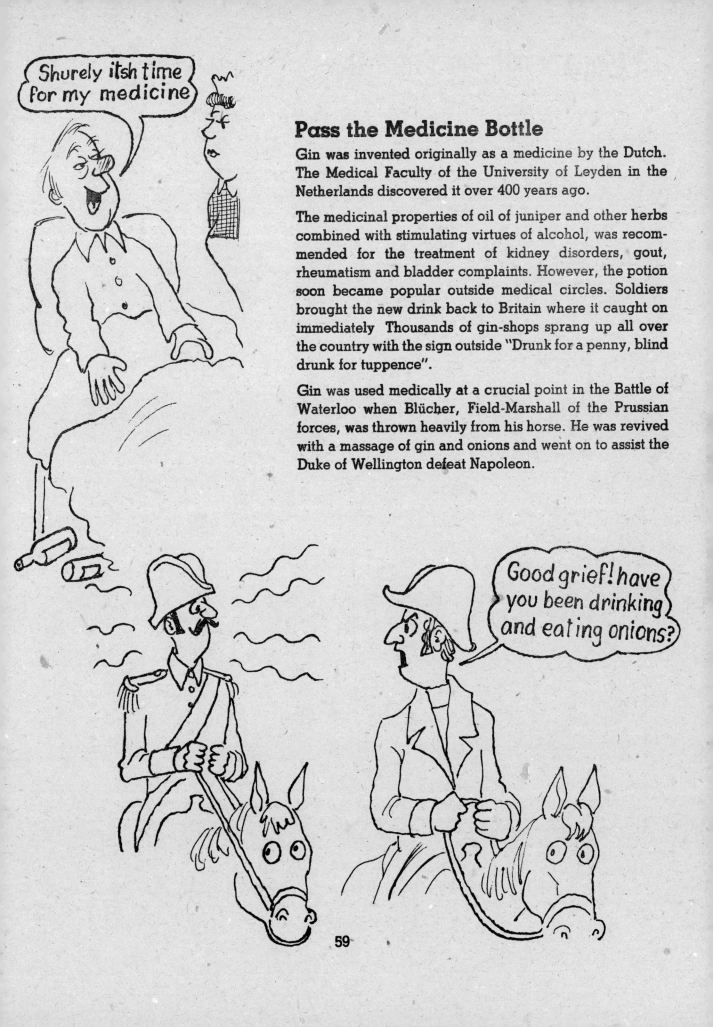

Pass the Medicine Bottle

Gin was invented originally as a medicine by the Dutch. The Medical Faculty of the University of Leyden in the Netherlands discovered it over 400 years ago.

The medicinal properties of oil of juniper and other herbs combined with stimulating virtues of alcohol, was recommended for the treatment of kidney disorders, gout, rheumatism and bladder complaints. However, the potion soon became popular outside medical circles. Soldiers brought the new drink back to Britain where it caught on immediately Thousands of gin-shops sprang up all over the country with the sign outside "Drunk for a penny, blind drunk for tuppence".

Gin was used medically at a crucial point in the Battle of Waterloo when Blücher, Field-Marshall of the Prussian forces, was thrown heavily from his horse. He was revived with a massage of gin and onions and went on to assist the Duke of Wellington defeat Napoleon.

SHORTEST WAR EVER

WHEN THE SULTAN OF ZANZIBAR, SEYID KHALID BIN BARGASH, DECLARED WAR ON GREAT BRITAIN AT 9·0AM. AUG 27TH 1898, BRITISH WARSHIPS IN THE AREA OPENED FIRE ON THE SULTAN'S PALACE. 38 MINUTES LATER THE SULTAN FLED AND THE WAR WAS OVER. THE ZANZIBAR BATTLE-SHIP "GLASGOW" WAS SUNK AND 500 SOLDIERS KILLED OR WOUNDED.

LADY RALEIGH,

WIDOW OF SIR WALTER RALEIGH, CARRIED HER HUSBAND'S EMBALMED HEAD WHEREVER SHE WENT UNTIL SHE DIED 29 YEARS AFTER HIS EXECUTION. HER SON, CAREW, CONTINUED THE TRADITION UNTIL HIS DEATH IN 1666 WHEN HIS FATHER'S HEAD WAS INTERRED WITH HIM.

JACK BURKE AND AMERICAN NEGRO ANDY BOWEN FOUGHT FOR 110 ROUNDS — 7 HOURS 19 MINUTES, IN NEW ORLEANS APRIL 6. 1893, WHEN THE REFEREE STOPPED THE FIGHT DECLARING IT A "NO CONTEST".

Unique Duel

In 15th century Franconia, if a woman's reputation was sullied by a man she was at liberty to challenge him to a duel — but what a duel!

A ring was formed by spectators around a hole about 3 ft deep. The man, armed only with a club, stood in the hole. The woman had a stone weighing a pound tied up in a handkerchief and attached to a slender willowy stick. The woman had a space measuring 10 ft in diameter in which to manouvre and attack.

If the man, in attempting to strike the woman, touched the ground with either his hand or his arm it counted as one error. Three such errors and he was declared defeated, executed and buried in the hole in which he stood.

However, if he succeeded in thwarting the attacks of the woman or managed to disarm her he was declared the victor, and the woman was then sentenced to death and buried alive.

Döppelganger

The Döppelganger, your own psychic double, has puzzled scientists and researchers for centuries. Although reports come from all over the world, especially Germany, where the name originates, it rarely occurs in Britain. In Britain it is known as the Fetch, and the superstition is that if you meet it, it is an omen of death, but in many cases it could be regarded as a guardian angel.

One such case recorded, having happened to American, Alex B. Griffith, in 1944 an infantry sergeant in the US Army in France, not just once but twice. One late summer's afternoon he was in charge of a patrol near Rennes. Everything seemed quiet as the patrol made its way along a dusty, narrow road.

Suddenly, a figure appeared in the road a few yards ahead, the sergeant gasped in amazement, the figure was an exact duplicate of himself, even to the strip of sticking plaster on his chin.

His double was frantically waving his arms, quite obviously warning him to go back.

Griffith and the patrol retreated and as they did so a Jeep roared past, going up the road. After a few seconds the sound of a Spandau machine-gun shattered the quiet and the Jeep crashed off the road, spilling its occupants on to the road, all dead. There was a hidden German machine-gun nest up the road. If the patrol had continued along the road, they would have been wiped out.

Some twenty years on, Griffith had another Döppelganger experience. He was now married with two children

In June, 1964, the family were on a camping holiday in the Laurentians in Canada. The weather was fine but the wind was very gusty. As the family walked in single file through the trees, the wind swayed the treetops alarmingly.

As they came to a clearing it happened again — there stood the same figure that he had seen twenty years before. It looked just the way it had looked, combat uniform, helmet, even to the plaster on the chin, and it was giving the same message — go back! Griffith needed no second telling and about-turned his family at the double. As he did, there came a loud cracking, splintering of wood, a loud crash and a swirl of dust as a huge tree smashed into the earth, where Alex and family had been a few seconds before.

Alex is now an executive with an insurance company.

Much less useful was the Döppelganger of schoolmistress, Emile Sagée. She taught at a school for young girls, the Pensionnat de Neurvelcke near the Baltic port of Riga. The principal was a Monsieur Buck.

She had not been at the school long before strange things began to happen. Her pupils would often claim to have seen their teacher in two places at the same time.

One day in class, Miss Sagée was writing on the blackboard when the class suddenly started to scream — there were two Miss Sagées side by side.

The real Miss Sagée was writing on the blackboard with a piece of chalk — her double imitated all her movements except that it had no chalk. During meal times, her double was often seen standing behind her as she ate, imitating her every movement.

It was so unnerving to staff and pupils that eventually the principal had to ask Miss Sagée (and her Döppelganger) to leave.

She went to stay with her sister-in-law and her young children. The children weren't a bit put off by the double and would tell people that they had two Aunt Emilies.

Another case of a protective Döppelganger happened in Berlin. A professor of theology was walking down a street on his way home when he saw a figure on the other footpath that looked vaguely familiar, then he realised with a start that it was his double.

The professor quickened his step but the psychic double kept pace with him. He turned down side streets in an effort to shake off his eerie companion across the street. He thought he had until he turned the corner opposite his house and saw the figure pressing his front door bell.

The maid opened the door and admitted his double. The professor watched the candle which the double was carrying pass each window as it went upstairs to his room.

He crossed the road and raced up to his room. Just as he reached his door he heard a loud crash from within. Opening the door, he was met by a cloud of dust — the whole ceiling had collapsed into the room.

But for his Döppelganger the professor could have been seriously injured or even killed.

Statistically, it's very unlikely to happen to you but if it does, perhaps it means to save your life, you never know.

★ ★ ★ ★ ★ ★ ★

Falling Stars

Danzig Municipal Art Museum was very proud of its collection of art. Amongst them hung two paintings by famous artists, Breughel the Elder and Van Dyck, that is until the Breughel mysteriously fell off the wall in 1972. To the consternation of the museum staff, it was found that it was not the famous original but a picture cut from a magazine. After a panic examination, it was also found that the Van Dyck was also a reproduction from a magazine.

It remains a mystery as to when the pictures were switched, though a scientific examination of the frames and magazine cuttings showed that they had been hanging in the gallery for about ten years before the theft was discovered.

The missing masterpieces were worth around a cool half million pounds.

JAILHOUSE POP

ARRESTED IN 1690 ON A POLITICAL OFFENCE JOHN BERNARDINI WAS KEPT IN NEWGATE PRISON WITHOUT TRIAL FOR 46 YEARS. DURING HIS IMPRISONMENT HE MARRIED, AND FATHERED TEN CHILDREN.

A CUBIC SQUARE FOOT

OF SOLID GOLD WEIGHS ALMOST HALF-A-TON AND ONE OUNCE OF IT CAN BE DRAWN INTO A FINE WIRE 50 MILES LONG OR BEATEN INTO A 100 SQ.FT. SHEET.

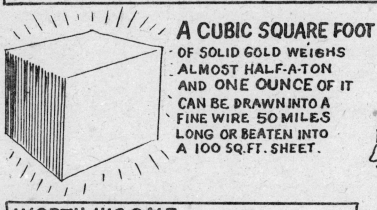

WORTH HIS SALT

PART OF A ROMAN SOLDIER'S PAY WAS MADE IN SALT KNOWN AS 'SALARIUM'. THAT'S WHY PAY OF TODAY IS KNOWN AS A SALARY.

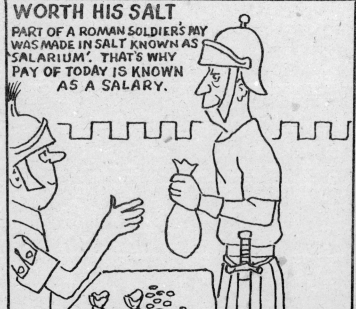

LITTLE GIANTKILLER

THE LITTLE URCHIN FISH - LESS THAN A FOOT LONG - IS A SHARK KILLER. ITS BODY IS COVERED IN SPINY POINTS AND WHEN SWALLOWED BY ITS ENEMY CAN DISTEND ITSELF INTO A DEADLY SPIKY BALL - IT THEN BORES AND EATS ITS WAY OUT THROUGH THE SHARK'S STOMACH AND ESCAPES

AN AVERAGE MAN CONSUMES ALMOST A TON OF FOOD AND DRINK IN A YEAR.

? ? ? ? ? ? ? ? ? ? ?

Superman

You don't know your own strength. It's a fact. Your super-strength first needs something to unchain it. Inside every-one is a super being waiting to get out.

Suppose you are suddenly faced with a dire emergency, what happens? Five major glands go into super-drive. They are the pituitary, your stomach glands, your thymus, your white blood cells and the adrenal glands. All combine to pour adrenalin into the body to meet the emergency.

At one time a live bomb — weighing 200 lbs — dropped on the deck of an aircraft carrier. At once, a short, slim sailor dashed to it, picked it up and carried it to the side and threw it overboard. When challenged to do the same next day with a similar bomb with the fuse removed, he couldn't even budge it!

In another instance, doctors tell of a young, intensely patriotic naval officer who went to sea for the first time on an armed merchant ship in 1942. He was given sealed, top-secret battle plans to deliver to fleet headquarters. The captain suggested that the envelope should be placed in the ship's safe. The safe was of cast iron, 4 ft high and riveted to the deck deep inside the ship.

One night the young officer was startled out of his sleep by the urgent clamour of the submarine alarm. He shot from his bunk and sprinted to the safe-room. It was only when he got there that he realised that only the captain knew the combination of the safe. Without more ado he wrenched the safe from its floor-bolts, heaved it on to his shoulder, raced up the companion way and placed it before the astonished captain.

The submarine alert turned out to be only a drill. It needed four hefty sailors to carry the safe back. None of them could even move it on his own!

The same sort of thing seems to be happening in sports. At one time to run a mile in 4 minutes seemed impossible, but how many times has the record been shattered since? One wonders when the limit for breaking records will be reached.

Vera Petrova

Vera Petrova of Ulyansk, Russia, is one of perhaps only a dozen people in the world who can "see" through their skin.

When Vera is blindfolded — but only then — she can actually "see" the contents of her father's iron safe by touching the door with her hands. She can also identify the people in a photograph by standing on it in her stockinged feet, a book can be "read" by touching the text, and she can distinguish colours by touch. Yet, if Vera's skin comes into contact with water, she loses the ability of her "skin sight". No-one can explain why.

Experts are working on the phenomenon in the hope that a way may be found to help blind people see.

Indian writer Ved Mehta, who became totally blind at the age of three after having meningitis, could cycle through the streets of Bombay as if he had full sight. Later, he studied at Balliol College, Oxford, and played a good game of chess with his fellow students and found his way around the city streets without the aid of a guide dog or a white stick. Mehta has what he calls "facial vision", he sees with the skin of his face.

Amazing sight of an entirely different kind is possessed by Veronica Seider of Germany who was born with eyesight twenty times more powerful than normal! When she was a student at Stuttgart University, she astounded a group of professors with a demonstration of her remarkable powers by writing twenty verses of a poem on a piece of paper the size of her thumb nail.

MIRIN DAJO
THE WONDERFUL ONE

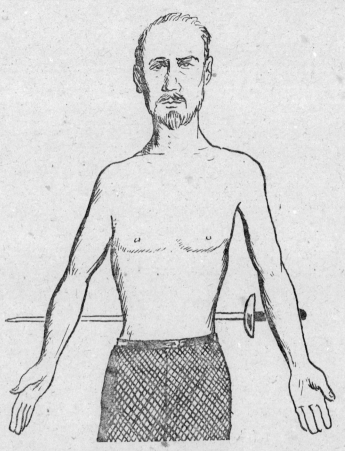

The slim Dutchman stood calmly whilst his assistant thrust a long, slender sword blade right through his **body** from back to front. Several people in the audience fainted but Mirin Dajo walked around, **transfixed** by the sword until it was carefully withdrawn and The Wonderful One continued living.

He did this 500 times in his life, sometimes the sword penetrated him from back to front; sometimes from **side** to side.

Mirin Dajo, which in Esperanto means "Wonderful One", was born in 1913 and had always been **fascinated** by the powers of Yoga and the hypnotic control practised by Indian fakirs and when he first **started** to give public demonstrations, his body was already scarred with the marks of the sword. He **claimed** to have supernormal powers and gave these demonstrations to publicise his mission to found a **World** Brotherhood of Peace. Just after World War II, newsreels of his amazing feat were shown in **many** countries with the same result of people fainting in the audience. To quash any suggestion of **trickery** he appeared before a committee of doctors and was X-rayed whilst the sword was through him. **This** proved conclusively that the blade passed clear through his body and it was no fake. But **Switzerland**, his adopted country, finally passed a special law which banned his public demonstrations.

He continued experimenting in private with sword swallowing and in May, 1948, he accidentally cut **his** throat — from the inside — this time he died.

WHO — WHY — WHERE — WHEN

Where is the biggest concrete construction? This is in the USA (where else!) in the state of Washington. The Grand Coulee Dam contains over 21,000,000 tons of concrete.

Why is the sky blue? Well, it isn't really, it's black! The colour effect is caused by the sun's rays striking the countless specks of dust in the earth's atmosphere, the blue rays being scattered farther than red. So it is the blue rays we see and leads us to believe the sky is of that colour.

If the air was completely dust-free, the sky would be quite dark relieved only by the brightness of the sun and the moon and stars which would always be visible.

Where did the swastica originate? Well, certainly not with the Nazis. The emblem adopted by the Nazis and .o become hated by millions, is found on Sumerian seals as long ago as 2850 BC. It also appears on Assyrian and Persian coins and the American Indian regarded it as a symbol of good luck for centuries.

Who Stocks the Most Book Titles?

W. & G. Foyle in London has 30 miles of shelves and has the most titles.

The world's largest second hand bookshop is in Wales, it is run by Richard Booth (Booksellers) Ltd, in Hay-on-Wye, Powys. It stocks 900,000 to 1,100,000 books.

Where is there a lake that sings? At Battacaloa, Sri Lanka, here there is a salt-water lake which on calm nights, especially when there is a full moon, emits clear and musical notes. The 'singing' appears to come from the bottom of the lake and, although no entirely satisfactory explanation has been given, it is believed the culprit is a certain kind of shellfish which inhabits the lake.

* * * * *

What king had 413 beds? The king of the beds was Louis XIV of France. The elaborately carved and gilded beds were dotted about his kingdom so that wherever he travelled he could always sleep in his own bed. The most magnificent was the great bed in the Palace of Versailles. This had velvet curtains with the "Triumph of Venus" woven in gold. His second wife, Madame de Maintenon, who was a religious bigot, had this pagan subject replaced by the "Sacrifice of Abraham".

Whose been sleeping in my bed?

WHO — WHY — WHERE —WHEN

What country has most telephones? Of the 400,000,000 telephones in use in the world today, almost 40% are in the United States but the country with the most 'phones in proportion to its population is the tiny nation of Monaco with 825 'phones for every 1,000 persons! The small country of Bhutan is at the other end of the scale with only one 'phone for every 2,000 persons. By 1900, a quarter of a century after the telephone was invented, there were still less than two million of them in the entire world!

When was one year only 354 days long? The year was 1752, when the New Style or Gregorian calendar was adopted in England. The days between September 2 and 14 were omitted because the calendar then in use containing 365¼ days had got 11 days behind the seasons as determined by the sun. Crowds of people gathered, shouting, "Give us back our eleven days!" especially the ones whose birthdays fell within the missing days. They thought their lives had been shortened.

Who discovered vaccination? This honour goes to Dr Edward Jenner (1749–1823) who was talking to a patient, a milkmaid, when she came out with the chance remark that she could not catch smallpox as she had already had cowpox, an infection which is caught from handling cows' udders and, she declared, rendered her immune to the dreaded smallpox responsible in those days for the death or disfigurement of thousands of people. Jenner had never heard of this idea and began experimenting with cowpox germs until he had perfected an effective safeguard against smallpox by inoculating healthy people with cowpox germs and then germs of smallpox. The latter disease did not take.

When his discovery was published, honours were heaped on him from all quarters. Germany celebrated his birthday as a holiday and in Russia the first child to be vaccinated was named "Vaccinov" and given free education.

Napoleon, then at war with England, set free an English prisoner at Jenner's request because, he said, "We can refuse him nothing".

How did nicknames originate? Primitive man regarded his name as his personal and private property and as such was rarely, if ever, to be used. To his friends he was known, in old English, by an eke name, an added name, careless pronunciation turned this into "a nickname".

WHO — WHY — WHERE — WHEN

What statesman died in the cause of science? Francis Bacon, Baron Verulam (1561—1626) the celebrated philosopher and essayist, Lord Chancellor of England under James I, was always keenly interested in scientific matters. One day he caught a cold while trying to stuff a chicken with snow to test its refrigerating qualities. He developed bronchitis and died some weeks later.

Why is sudden fear called "panic"? The word is derived directly from the name of the Greek god Pan, protector of sheep and patron of shepherds. His uncouth and awesome appearance struck terror in all who saw him causing "panic fear". He was always depicted having a horned head and the hindquarters of a goat. All the strange noises coming from the hills and valleys were attributed to him. Pan, whose name signifies "everything", was originally one of the eight great gods of Egyptian mythology.

Who made the first potato crisps? According to all reports the crisp originated in Saratoga, New York, around 1865, owing to a very finicky diner at a guest house. The chef had made a batch of thinly-sliced potatoes but one guest kept sending his back demanding thinner slices.

The exasperated chef cut a potato wafer thin and popped them into the oil, and so created the first potato crisps!

The first factory built solely for the production of crisps opened in Albany, New York, in 1925.

? ?

Well, thin enough yet?

Why would a penny dropped off a high place, such as Blackpool Tower, become a killer? When an object is dropped from a great height it gathers momentum or increasing force the farther it falls and can strike the ground with a greater force than a heavier object falling a shorter distance. So our penny, striking a person in the right place, could be a deadly missile.

? ?

Heads, I think.

Would that be Mr. and Mrs John Smith?

Which king earned his living as a schoolmaster? Louis Philippe (1773–1850) who fled to Switzerland during the French Revolution, taught mathematics in a college at Reichenau under an assumed name. He ascended the throne of France after the revolution of 1830 and abdicated in 1848, when he and his queen fled the country in disguise with the highly original name of "Mr and Mrs Smith". He was absolutely unfitted for the task of ruling France and gave it up as a bad job.

WHO — WHY — WHERE — WHEN

Who was the masked prisoner? The well-known novel "The Man in the Iron Mask" by French writer Alexandre Dumas, was based on a real incident in history.

In 1669, a prisoner, sentenced to life imprisonment, was turned over to the warden of a French prison, the difference was this prisoner was masked, not in iron but in a black velvet hood. He was to be allowed all sorts of privileges not allowed to other prisoners, but **he** was never allowed to remove his mask.

...and I'd like the steak medium rare, oh, and another bottle of wine

The very special prisoner spent 34 years in jail, dying there without anyone knowing his identity or what his crime was and still wearing his mask. But people speculated that he was in fact the twin brother of the French king, Louis XIV, imprisoned to avoid any dispute over the throne.

Where is there a country which bans females? The answer is Athos, a piece of land jutting out from Greece into the Aegean Sea and populated entirely by monks. The monks forbade females from their land in the 11th century and it's only recently that hens and she-cats have been allowed to provide eggs and keep the mice down. Probably the only man in history who never set eyes on a woman lived in Athos. The monk, Mihailo Tolotos, lost his mother the day he was born and was taken to one of the 20 monastries the next day. He spent the rest of his life there without ever seeing a female.

What fool said you never miss what you've never had?

Whose been moving my type about?

Who printed the first book with moveable type? A German named Gutenberg holds this distinction. He printed 200 copies of the Bible in 1455 by this method. Of these, only 21 complete copies are known to exist today. One of them was sold in an auction in 1978 for about 1½ million pounds, the most expensive book ever printed and yet the printer died a pauper!

WHO — WHY — WHERE — WHEN

? ? ? ? ? ? ?

What is the largest snake? Rival claimants for this title are the anaconda found in South America and the recitulated python of Malaysia. Both attain 30 feet in length. They are not poisonous but kill their prey by coiling round it and crushing it to death.

It's alright, it says here they're not poisonous.

Here you are - you can have my homework too.

What was the burning of the books? In 212 BC Ch'in Shih Huang Tih one of China's greatest emperors, a builder of the Great Wall, styled himself as the "First Emperor" and decreed that history should begin with him. To ensure that aim and obliterate the past, he burned all books, with the exception of a select few on subjects such as agriculture, medicine, etc. Vast numbers of valuable works were destroyed and it was only through the efforts of a few brave teachers and scholars that any of the earlier literature of China survived. It was nearly a century and a half before it was safe to bring the surviving books from their hiding place.

Where is there a tree that gives milk? In Venezuela is a tree the sap of which is sweet and creamy like milk, the locals "milk" the Cowtree, as it is known, by making cuts into the bark and collecting the fluid which exudes, in little cups. Scientists report it as being almost as nutritious as cows' milk.

? ? ? ?
? ? ? ?
? ? ? ?

? ? ? ?
? ? ? ?
? ? ? ?

Where is there a statue to a cow? There is a statue of a cow in Ontario, Canada. It was erected by the proud owner of a prize-winning milker called "Springbank Snow Countess". Average cows give about 530 gallons of milk a year. Champion cows yield over 3,400 gallons a year.

Which is the Largest Brewery in Europe?
This title goes to the Guinness Brewery of Dublin, Ireland.

WHO — WHY — WHERE — WHEN

Who named electricity? Although electricity is thought of as a modern thing it was a doctor to Queen Elizabeth I who first coined the word. William Gilbert (1544—1603), used the Greek word electron which means amber because, as men had known for many years, a piece of amber rubbed on cloth acts as a magnet to small light objects. Actually, Gilbert called this power of attraction vis electrica; the word electricity first appeared in print in 1650.

★ ★ ★ ★

I'll be glad when its winter.

What country has the highest rainfall? No, not Britain, but the southern slopes of the Khasi Hills in eastern India. At Cherrapunji in Assam, an average annual rainfall of 425 ins, is recorded and over 900 ins. has been recorded in one year. Almost all this vast quantity falls during the summer, the rest of the year being practically rainless!

★ ★ ★ ★

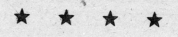

★ ★ ★ ★

When was soap first used? The Latin writer Pliny (23—79) wrote that soap was an invention of the Gauls who used it to slick down their hair. It wasn't known to the Greeks and Romans until fairly late in their history. Oils and ashes of plants were used for domestic uses and fullers earth for laundering. In Pompeii, smothered in volcanic ash in 79 AD, was found a complete soap making factory with the remains of soap still in the vats.

But I can't wash my neck, soap hasn't been invented yet!

WHO — WHY — WHERE — WHEN

Where did the metric system originate? The system had its birth during the French Revolution in France. It was based upon the metre being one ten-millionth part of the shortest distance along the earth's surface between the pole and the equator. The metre is divided into 100 centimetres, and the metric system of weights is based upon the weight of one cubic centimetre of water. I don't know why they bothered.

Right, citizen, take this tape-measure and nip up to the North Pole.

Who was history's biggest glutton? Vitellus, Emperor of Rome in 69 AD spent over £1,200 a day on food alone. He was capable of downing 1,000 oysters a day as well as vast quantities of other delicacies. After a short reign he was deposed by the Roman citizens, driven to revolt by the excesses of their emperor, and finished as food for the fishes of the River Tiber where the people dumped his body.

That's 1,001, better stand by with the bi-carb.

CONFUCIUS, HE SAYS...
THERE ARE 40,000 DIRECT DESCENDANTS
OF CONFUCIUS (551-478 B.C.) FAMOUS CHINESE
PHILOSOPHER, LIVING IN CHINA AT THE
PRESENT TIME.

MULAI ISHAEL
EMPEROR OF MOROCCO (1646-1727)
WAS THE FATHER OF 888 CHILDREN!
HIS SONS NUMBERED 540 AND FORMED
A WHOLE REGIMENT IN THE ROYAL ARMY.

THE BARBER'S GUILD PRESENTED
EACH MOTHER WITH A GIFT OF A
SILVER MIRROR FOR EACH GIRL AND
A GOLD RAZOR FOR A BOY.

TINY 'ROO
A NEW-BORN
KANGAROO
MEASURES ONLY
THREE-QUARTERS
OF AN INCH BUT
STAYS IN ITS
MOTHER'S POUCH
UNTIL FULLY
DEVELOPED.

THE WORLD'S RAREST PLANT
IS A TYPE OF SILVERSWORD
WHICH IS ONLY KNOWN TO
GROW IN THE EXTINCT
VOLCANO CRATER ON AN
ISLAND IN HAWAII.

What's in a name? Well there's one young chap in Italy who was given no fewer than sixteen Christian names by his proud parents. The initials alone take up a good deal of space. They are: S.F.H.K.O.L.R. W.U.T.Z.A.P.Y.B.E.M. Too bad if he ever has to write his full name on some government form!

The other end of the scale is a Belgian businessman whose full name is Anton O. Another short surname is the Irish Ek. A once-famous explorer was named John Ek.

The name Mr Blue Murder belongs to a respectable citizen living in Augusta, USA, his address is in Dead Man's Alley, the combination raises quite a few eyebrows as you may imagine.

Other unusual names seem to attract one another. In England, a Mr Young married a Miss Innocent and in Gloucester, a Mr Rolling Stone took as his wife a Miss Emma Moss.

In Ohio, USA a lady has a mouth-full of a name but she boasts that she can say it in one breath, it is Miss Cerasacasadannovaladetzalazambra. You try pronouncing, never mind saying it, all in one breath! I wonder if she gets many letters.

Boney Tale

There are six million skeletons buried in the catacombs under Paris. But the catacombs weren't built as cemeteries, they were originally quarries used by the Romans over 2,000 years ago.

Many of the remains were victims of the French revolution, but most of the bones come from cemeteries which had to be closed down for health reasons in the eighteenth century.

When Picasso was a poor student in Paris, he painted life-sized pictures of furniture on the bare walls of his room. So realistic were the paintings that his landlord had to touch the walls to convince himself that the furniture wasn't in fact real.

The students of Rembrandt fooled him by painting a silver coin on the studio floor. He bent to pick it up but couldn't, when he heard the chuckles of the art class, he realised a joke had been played on him.

Whistler had great fun painting flies on windows and mirrors and watching people trying to swat them. But one of his jokes had a tragic ending. A patron of his lent him a house in which to spend a holiday, Whistler painted life-sized peacocks on the morocco leather covered walls and when the owner saw the peacocks on his expensively covered walls, he had a heart attack and died.

JOKE PAINTING KILLED ARTIST'S PATRON

POPULAR VEG.

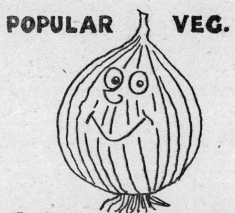

THE MOST WIDELY USED VEGETABLE IN THE WORLD IS THE **ONION**. MORE THAN 20 BILLION POUNDS ARE PRODUCED EACH YEAR!

ISLAND OF DOGS

HOW DID THE CANARY ISLANDS GET THEIR NAME? NO, NOT FROM THE LITTLE YELLOW BIRDS BUT FROM THE ANCIENT ROMANS WHO, WHEN THEY LANDED THERE, FOUND MANY WILD DOGS RUNNING ABOUT, SO THEY NAMED IT INSULAE CANARIAE "ISLAND OF THE DOGS"

SEWARD'S FOLLY

'SEWARD'S FOLLY' WAS THE DERISIVE NAME GIVEN TO ALASKA WHEN AMERICAN SEC.Y OF STATE BOUGHT THE APPARENTLY USELESS PIECE OF FROZEN WASTELAND FROM RUSSIA FOR $7·2 MILLION OR 2 CENTS AN ACRE. SINCE 1896 GOLD OIL AND GAS HAVE BEEN FOUND THERE WORTH MANY, MANY TIMES THE ORIGINAL PRICE.

THE BIG BANG

WHEN THE VOLCANO ON THE PACIFIC ISLAND OF KRAKATOA EXPLODED IN 1883, 37,000 PEOPLE PERISHED AND 200,000,000 CUBIC FEET OF LAND WAS BLOWN TO SMITHEREENS AND MANY SHIPS SUNK BY THE RESULTING TIDAL WAVES, MANY WERE FOUND WASHED MILES INLAND.
FOR MANY YEARS AFTER THE BIG BANG THE DUST IN THE ATMOSPHERE GAVE BEAUTIFUL SUNSETS THE WORLD OVER.

IT'S BEAN RAINING

In this century it has rained fish on Washington, jellyfish in Melbourne, frogs in Wigan, pilchards in Cardiff and even frozen beans in Los Angeles.

Many weird things have fallen from the skies over the centuries, such as the black rain which fell on the fishermen off Cornwall in 1959, and in the same year, washing, hanging on the lines in the back gardens of Huddersfield, was treated to a shower of indelible red rain. In 1950 a blue kind of fruit squash fell in Leicestershire. One theory is that elderberries were stripped off the trees by a freak whirlwind many miles away, squashed in the clouds and dropped.

How does anything but water fall from the sky? Water spouts, whirlwinds or even just gusty winds can suck dust, fishes, etc. high into the atmosphere, sometimes 20,000–40,000 ft high, and carry them many miles before they are released when it rains.

Sign Here

Autographs are big business these days. In America, the Charles Hamilton New York Gallery of Written Documents, has an annual turnover of half-a-million pounds. The late President J. F. Kennedy hardly ever hand-signed a document, he used a mechanical device to reproduce his signature and consequently a genuine John F. Kennedy signature would bring up to £25,000 today.

Emperor Napoleon left a legacy of £8,750,000,000 in the form of 250,000 autographs, each one is worth £35,000. Adolf Hitler's is worth five times as much as Churchill's. It seems villain's autographs bring more money than others; John Wilkes Booth, assassin of Abraham Lincoln, brings £500 — that of his brother Edwin, best known American actor of his day, fetches a mere £25.

Your name is worth more when you're dead than before, since Elvis Presley died his signature fetches over £250, while Martin Luther King's is worth as much as Abraham Lincoln's. Probably the most expensive signature is that of Button Gwinnet. As a representative of Georgia he signed the American Declaration of Independence, July 4th, 1776. Experts say if it came on the market it would fetch £104,000.

THE **KOALA**, A MARSUPIAL MAMMAL FOUND ONLY IN AUSTRALIA AND COMMONLY CALLED THE NATIVE BEAR, IS NOT A MEMBER OF THE BEAR FAMILY.

IT SPENDS MOST OF ITS LIFE UP THE BLUE-GUM OR EUCALYPTUS TREES FEEDING EXCLUSIVELY ON THE LEAVES FROM WHICH IT OBTAINS BOTH FOOD AND MOISTURE.

A CROW INDIAN GREW HIS HAIR **25** FT. LONG.

PURE-BLOODED RED INDIANS OFTEN GREW HAIR 10 OR 12 FEET LONG YET HAD LITTLE OR NO FACIAL HAIR.

SNAIL EGGS!

THE GIANT LAND SNAIL OF AFRICA, WHICH HAS A SHELL **7** INCHES LONG, LAYS EGGS SIMILAR IN SHAPE AND APPEARANCE TO BIRD'S EGGS.

The Sausage Duel

Bismarck, the famous German statesman was involved in a duel with a certain professor. The statesman was highly skilled with sword and pistol and, as the professor was not, Bismarck gave him the choice of weapons. At the appointed time and place the professor arrived carrying two sausages. One, he said, was harmless and the other was stuffed with meat which contained deadly germs.

He told Bismarck to choose one and eat it, he would eat the other. Bismarck angrily declined and the duel was called off. Bismarck fought 28 duels as a student at the University of Göttingen.

Students at University College, London, soon get used to the longest staying occupant. He is the dressed skeleton of Jeremy Bentham, who died in 1832, and has been displayed in a glass-fronted mahogany case in the University since 1850.

Bentham's mummified head rests in an oak chest nearby the seated figure, the head on the skeleton is wax.

When Bentham wrote his will in May 1832, he requested that his body should be used for medical science and his skeleton re-assembled and placed in a case. Shortly after he died at the grand old age of 84 and, in accordance with his request, his body was taken to Webb Street School of Anatomy and Medicine where a lecture was given on the human frame by an old friend of Bentham's, Dr Southwood Smith.

The body was dissected and afterwards the skeleton was dressed and the clothes were padded with cotton wool, wood, hay, and paper ribbon.

Until 1850, Bentham's skeleton was kept at Dr Smith's consulting rooms but was re-housed at University College when Dr Smith moved to new premises.

Jeremy Bentham was a social reformer in the 18th and early 19th century and one of his wishes was that a university should be created in London free of religious or political influences. He was instrumental in bringing about the abolition of transportation, the protection of inventors' rights and the extension of the poor laws amongst many other good things.

TIME TWINS

Astrologers put forward the theory that there are many "time-twins" in the world, that is, people who are born under the same position under the sun, moon and stars, and the fact that their characters, abilities, traits and even their appearances are similar.

Probably the best known example of this is that of George III and one Samuel Hemming, ironmonger.

Both born June 4th, 1738. Sam set up in business the day George became King. Both married on September 8th, 1761. Each had nine sons and six daughters, became ill and had accidents at the same time, and both died January 29th, 1820.

"Time-twins", they say, frequently crop up among ordinary people but are rarely recorded.

Talked to Death

A death certificate from a Canadian doctor in Edmonton in 1925 gave the reason or contributory cause of death as "Talked to death". He claimed that his patient would probably have made a recovery but for the fact that he had been bothered by relatives anxious about the contents of his will.

GEORGE I OF ENGLAND (REIGNED 1714-27)
RULER OF HANOVER FROM 1698, NEVER LEARNED TO SPEAK THE LANGUAGE OF HIS NEW SUBJECTS-ENGLISH

TRAILER TAIL
A CERTAIN BREED OF SHEEP IN THE EAST STORES FAT IN ITS TAIL IN MUCH THE SAME WAY AS A CAMEL DOES IN ITS HUMP. THE TAIL GROWS SO BIG THAT THE SHEPHERDS FIT THEM WITH LITTLE CARTS TO PREVENT THEM DRAGGING ON THE GROUND - TALK ABOUT LITTLE BO-PEEP!

GERM WARFARE-IN THE MIDDLE AGES
SOLDIERS, BESIEGING TOWNS AND CASTLES IN THE MIDDLE AGES, USED TO CATAPULT DECAYING CARCASSES OF ANIMALS OVER THE DEFENSIVE WALLS TO SPREAD DISEASE.

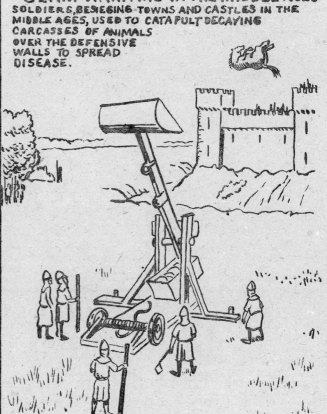

FISHY DISGUISE
THE LEAF FISH, WHICH LIVES IN THE RIVERS OF SOUTH AMERICA, LOOKS EXACTLY LIKE A DEAD LEAF, THIS ENABLES IT TO DRIFT SLOWLY TOWARDS ANY SMALLER FISH THEN MAKE A LIGHTNING DART ON ITS PREY.

RASPUTIN - THE EVIL MONK

The generals and noblemen of Tsarist Russia watched the black-bearded figure in monk's habit, seated in the guest of honour's place at the head of the banquet table in the palace of Prince Yussupoff, for this was the hated Rasputin, the monk who exerted such control over the Russian royal family, and they had planned to exterminate him.

Somehow the huge six-feet, six-inch monk seemed to know what was in their minds. Only a few weeks before he had told the Tsar's courtiers, "Yes, you all hate me! But our fates are bound together. Should I die none of you will survive me for long!"

He had also hinted more than once that he was in league with the Devil himself.

The Prince proposed a toast and Rasputin drained his glass in a gulp — a wine laced with a deadly poison. But he calmly poured himself another glass. The company watched in horror as the huge monk drained glass after glass of poisoned wine. He should have been in his death throes. It was obvious to them now that he did have satanic powers.

Prince Yussupoff rose, drew his revolver and fired at Rasputin at point-blank range. The monk stood up and advanced towards his executioners but finally slumped to the floor. They dragged the body to the river to push it through the ice; but suddenly the unholy monk began to crawl towards his attackers. They were about to run in panic when the monster collapsed and lay still. They pushed the body through a hole in the ice and hurried away, shivering, but not entirely with cold.

That happened in the December of 1916. Less than a year later Russia sued for peace with Germany and the country was torn by revolution.

The evil monk's prophecy had come true.

On Strike

In 1970 the 8 ton clock tower bell on the Guildhall, Portsmouth, began to strike non-stop. In fact it struck continuously for 2,225 times until 3 am, when an engineer arrived to put right the short circuit which had started the striking.

Silent bells hung in Carlisle Cathedral for 180 years. They were sentenced to everlasting silence for ringing out a welcome to Bonnie Prince Charlie during the Stuart rebellion. They remained silent until the sentence was "repealed" in 1925.

The church bell of Uglich in Russia was punished for ringing the alarm when the son of Ivan the Terrible was assassinated, on the orders of Ivan, in 1591. The bell was sentenced to 300 strokes of the lash and exile in Siberia for 300 years. The bell was returned in 1892.

Another kind of bell brought the house down, literally, when a Hamburg man rang the door-bell of a neighbour's house in 1955, the place blew-up. The middle-aged couple, whose house it was, had decided to commit suicide after the husband had learned he had an incurable illness. They had turned the gas on and a spark from the electric bell had ignited it and caused the explosion.

MASK OF DEATH

FAMOUS IRISH BEAUTY OF THE 18th. CENTURY, LADY MARIA COVENTRY, DIED THROUGH USING A PASTE TO ATTAIN THE FASHIONABLE WHITE SKIN OF THE PERIOD.

THE 'MAKE-UP' CONSISTED MAINLY OF DEADLY POISONOUS WHITE LEAD Died October 1760

SACRED TOOTH

IN THE TEMPLE OF THE SACRED TOOTH IN SRI LANKA, (CEYLON) IS A PIECE OF BONE WORSHIPPED BY OVER 400,000,000 PEOPLE — THE BONE IS BELIEVED BY THEM TO BE THE LEFT EYE-TOOTH OF BUDDHA.

ONE OF THE BITTEREST WINTERS IN ENGLAND OCCURRED IN 1708 WHEN EVEN BIRDS IN FLIGHT FELL FROZEN TO DEATH.

KING BILLY

WILLIAM III (1688-1702) OF ENGLAND, GRANDSON OF CHARLES I, WAS ALSO WILLIAM IV OF NORMANDY, WILLIAM III OF HOLLAND, WILLIAM II OF SCOTLAND AND WILLIAM I OF IRELAND.

The CRATER OF DIAMONDS

In the state of Arkansas, USA, is a 72 acre state-owned treasure field in which, for an entrance fee of just £2, tourists can search for diamonds.

In 1963, tourists out hunting for a valuable stone returned to their baby, whom they had left playing on a blanket near their car; they were disenchanted and empty-handed. When they looked at the shiny object that the baby was sucking, it turned out to be an 11.92 carat diamond worth £4,000.

A retired engineer, 62 year old Billy Johnson, was another who struck it lucky. On holiday in the area, he paid his £2 finders keepers fee and was amazed to find a walnut sized 16.37 carat gem lying on the surface. It turned out to be worth £50,000.

The DEALER of DEATH

During his long service as President of the Court of Sessions in Leipzig, Germany, from 1620 to 1666, he sentenced over 30,000 people to death, mainly for theft and witchcraft. About two thirds of these were women.

He made a point of attending the executions in person, to make sure that a dead dog and a rodent were buried with the body of the "witch".

To the judge, condemning five people a day to death was just an average day's work. He was proud of being a regular churchgoer and the fact that he had read the Bible from beginning to end fifty times during his lifetime.

Yet this insensitive man died of grief shortly after his pet dog died.

Featherweight Man

On June 20th, 1884, Reynard Beck, of Dexter, Kansas, USA hopped out of bed — but his feet never touched the floor — he just floated!

He had to pull himself down by grasping at pieces of heavy furniture. When he tried to walk he just trod air. He eventually came up with a solution to keep his feet on the ground, he tied lead fishing weights to his belt. But a couple of days later, Reynard's brother Frank called on him and was amazed to find him floating in mid-air.

Reynard told him what happened and Frank came up with the idea of making money out of the phenomenon.

They opened a side-show and created an immediate sensation, people suspected hidden wires or magnets to hold him up, but Reynard floated serenely on. Scientific investigators could find no reason for his weightlessness and were baffled.

The "gift" did have its disadvantages, he had to be strapped in his bed at night to prevent him finishing up on the ceiling and at meal times he had to be tied to a heavy chair.

People flocked to see "the man who could defy gravity" and paid the brothers well for the opportunity.

And then, as suddenly as it came, Beck's "gift" left him and he became a normal weight again, much to his relief. He retired to his home town and lived a normal life. No explanation has ever been given as to why this fantastic ability came and went as it did.

94

AUGUST - THE STRONGARM KING

KING AUGUST OF SAXONY AND POLAND (1670-1733) WAS KNOWN AS 'AUGUST THE STRONG' AND USED HIS 10 STONE VALET AS A WEIGHT IN HIS DAILY EXERCISES ON HIS PALACE BALCONY. HE WOULD LIFT THE MAN OVER THE PARAPET AND STRETCH AND BEND HIS ARMS BACK AND FORTH ~ SUSPENDING HIS "WEIGHT" OVER A 750 FT. DROP!

THE KING WAS ALSO THE FATHER OF 355 CHILDREN - ONLY ONE BEING LEGITIMATE AND WHO EVENTUALLY BECAME AUGUST III

SOME BAIT! EARTHWORMS 6 FT. LONG LIVE IN SOME PARTS OF AUSTRALIA.

Ouch!

In the Japan of old, dentists didn't use metal instruments to pull teeth — they used bare fingers. To extract a tooth, the dentist would hold the patient's head in such a way that his mouth was forced to remain open. Then in went thumb and fore-finger and out came the tooth.

Training started when the "would-be" dentist went to a special dental school where he would practise pulling wooden pegs from a board perforated with holes. For a start, the boards were of soft wood and the pegs not too tight. As the pupil progressed, the wooden boards got harder and the pegs fitted tighter. As time went on they gained skill and dexterity.

The boards were laid on the floor and the pupil had to extract the pegs, using thumb and fore-finger, without moving the board. When he could remove the tightest peg with this method he was judged to be fully qualified.

When a person had lost all his teeth he was fitted out with wooden false teeth which had pebbles for the front teeth and copper studs for the back teeth!

★ ★ ★ ★ ★

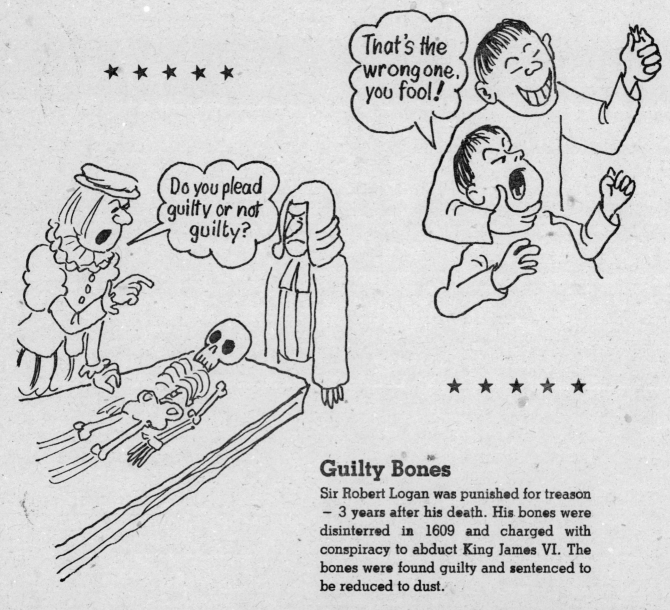

Guilty Bones

Sir Robert Logan was punished for treason — 3 years after his death. His bones were disinterred in 1609 and charged with conspiracy to abduct King James VI. The bones were found guilty and sentenced to be reduced to dust.

96

The MYSTERY OF THE GREEN CHILDREN

It was in the August of 1887 when Spanish peasants, busy in the fields gathering in the harvest, saw two children standing by a cavern in the hillside. Their clothing was of an unknown rubber-like material but strangest of all — their skin was green. They spoke in a language that the peasants from the village of Banjos, Spain, could not understand.

The local priest was called and he took them to magistrate Ricard da Calno, from nearby Barcelona.

They were offered a meal of meat and bread which they regarded with suspicion and didn't eat. For five days they ate nothing but when they saw a basket of raw beans, just gathered from the garden, the pair ate them with gusto. For four weeks they lived on beans and water but the boy, the younger of the two, began to wane and died.

The girl, aged about eight, living on beans and greenstuff, remained with da Calno and actually learned a little of the Spanish language. She told an amazing story of their world in which the sun was unknown and the light was always like twilight. When asked how they came from the cave, all she answered was that there was a loud bang and they had found themselves at the entrance to the "outside world".

The green colour of the little girl's skin and hair began to fade over the next five years but she hardly grew. Da Carlo kept her protected from the curious eyes of sightseers but did allow a doctor and a priest to examine and talk to her. Both men testified that the child's green colour was part of the flesh and not just a surface colouring.

Where had they come from? Nobody can say to this day. The little bodies are buried side by side in Banjos cemetery, a complete mystery.

NAMELESS ONE

The Kwakiutl Indians of British Columbia pawn their names if they need money. Until the debt is repaid, the borrower remains nameless.

Everyone should have a hobby-it keeps you going

Jose Caba Alvarez, of Manzanares, Spain, had a weird hobby — he attended funerals. Not just of friends or relatives but of the several thousands of people who had attended his father's funeral. In 40 years he attended 15,220 funerals starting in 1913.

MESSENGER OF DOOM

NED PEARSON, GRAVEDIGGER OF GRIMSBY, FOR 22 YEARS WAS KNOWN TO HAVE VISITED THE HOME OF HIS NEXT "CUSTOMER" SOME 24 HOURS BEFORE THE PERSON DIED!

TRAVELLING MAN

NORWEGIAN MENSON ERNST, WHO LIVED IN THE EARLY 19TH. CENTURY, MADE WHAT IS PROBABLY THE GREATEST CROSS-COUNTRY RUN OF ALL TIME.

STARTING FROM PARIS HE RAN THE 1,600 MILES TO MOSCOW IN JUST 13 DAYS. HE RAN ON ROADS LITTLE BETTER THAN CART TRACKS AND SWAM THIRTEEN RIVERS ON THE WAY. HE AVERAGED 120 MILES A DAY.

Look, No Hands!

COUNT MERAL, AN ITALIAN NOBLE-MAN, COULD PART HIS HAIR WITHOUT USING COMB OR FINGERS! HE RELIED SOLELY ON HIS HIGHLY DEVELOPED SCALP MUSCLES.

THE BATTLE OF HASTINGS.
OCT. 14.TH. 1066. WAS NOT AT HASTINGS BUT AT SENLAC HILL ABOUT SIX MILES AWAY.

KING IN PAWN
WHEN KING RICHARD II GOT MARRIED IN 1380 HE HAD TO PAWN THE CROWN JEWELS TO PAY FOR THE WEDDING

IN 1492...

"In fourteen hundred and ninety-two, Columbus sailed the ocean blue", is the rhyme familiar to generations of schoolchildren as an aid to remind them of the discoverer of the New World — but was he? At least ten nationalities now claim that distinction.

The Vikings are now believed to have reached North America, or Vinland as they called it, in the 10th century. Evidence has been found of their visits in Canada but the Irish contend that their monks were there converting the heathen four centuries before that.

The Welsh, too, claim to have colonised part of North America in the 12th century under the leadership of Prince Madoc. Indeed, early English settlers were surprised to find a tribe of fair skinned Indians who spoke an ancient form of the Welsh language. Even the Chinese have a story of a Buddhist, Hoei-Shin, who sailed to "the land of the painted people" in 499.

But the fact is that the Red Indian came originally from what we now know as Russia, some 15,000 years ago, crossing at what is now the Bering Strait. These first arrivals were primitive hunters and fishermen in search of new food supplies, they liked the new land they had found and spread throughout North America. So, in effect, native Russians were the discoverers of the New World.

Drowning Their Sorrows

In October 1814, three buildings collapsed, and 8 people died from drowning, drunkenness or fumes, when a huge vat of porter burst at Meux Brewery, Tottenham Court Road, London.

Many tenements surrounding the brewery were flooded by the 3,555 barrels of porter the vat had contained.

At the inquest, a verdict of "death by casualty" was returned.

100

STATUE ᴼꜰ ᴀ HEROINE

Towering above New York harbour, the Statue of Liberty has been a symbol of hope and freedom for millions of immigrants for nearly a century. The 305 ft statue and base was a gift from the people of France, money being raised by voluntary contributions of French citizens to mark the centenary of the American revolution in 1876.

She was inspired by an unknown girl shot down by the military whilst demonstrating for her own political freedom in the streets of Paris over 100 years ago. The sculptor, Frederic-Auguste Bartholdi, when asked to sculpt a giant statue, remembered the girl carrying a flaming torch when he saw her shot. A massive iron pylon embedded in the rock forms the backbone of the figure, inspired by the unknown French girl.

Facts About Liberty

The face is ten feet wide and forty people can stand in the interior of the head, the torch bearing arm is forty feet long and the torch platform can hold twelve people. The actual statue from foot to torch is 152 ft and weighs 450,000 lbs and stands on a 62 ft square base, the overall height is 305 ft 6 ins (nearly as high as St Paul's Cathedral) and erection was dedicated by President Grover Cleveland in 1886.

No E

The letter "E" is the most used in the English language, yet Ernest Vincent Wright wrote a book entitled, "Gadsby, a story of over 50,000 words without using the letter E."

To make sure that no "E's" accidently slipped into the text, the author tied down the E key on his typewriter.

About Hanging About

Inetta de Balsham, sentenced to be hanged for harbouring criminals in 1264, really did hang — from 9 am on Monday morning 'till sunrise on the following Thursday — yet she was still very much **alive** when she was cut down! When Henry III heard of her ordeal he granted her a royal pardon.

Another criminal, a Swiss, gained the reputation of being "the man they couldn't hang" — they **tried** alright — 13 times in fact, but with no effect. Only much later was it discovered that he had an **infection** that caused his windpipe to become as hard as bone, making it impossible to asphyxiate him.

But Ann Green, a servant girl sentenced to death in 1650 at Oxford for practising witchcraft, had **her** legs violently jerked while hanging. Then she was cut down and was jumped and trampled on, **after** which surgeons carried her off for dissection. They were about to start cutting her up when Ann **showed** a flicker of life. Fourteen hours later she was able to speak but could tell the doctors nothing of what **had** happened to her. "It is as if I had awoken from a deep sleep," she said.

Surprisingly, she did not have to face a further charge of sorcery but was granted a pardon, **she later** married and became the mother of three healthy children.

In 1705, a housebreaker named Smith was hanged at Tyburn and had been dangling for fifteen **minutes** when his reprieve came through. He was cut down, bled by a surgeon and was soon up and about, **a** much wiser man.

The case of John Lee, a murderer condemned to hang at Exeter Jail in 1895, was perhaps the **strangest** of all. Every time Lee stood on the trap it refused to work, yet each time the apparatus was **tested, it** worked perfectly

Lee's sentence was commuted to life imprisonment and after a few years he was released.

THE HUMAN MEDICAL LABORATORY

One June day in 1822, a young Canadian Army doctor, William Beaumont, received an emergency call to a French-Canadian fur trapper who had been accidentally shot at a nearby trading post. When the doctor saw the wound, a huge hole blasted out of the man's left side just below the ribs, he expected him to die at any moment but he stayed by his patient for the next 36 hours, changing the blood-soaked dressings. The trapper survived, but with an opening more than an inch wide, through flesh and muscle into the stomach.

The man, 18 year old Alexis St Martin, not only survived with the hole in his side but resumed his work as a trapper with no ill effects at all and remained perfectly healthy until he died at the age of 76.

He ate normally and throughout his life, doctors studied him and observed how food was digested through the hole in his stomach. St Martin's unique wound gave much hitherto unknown knowledge of how the digestive process worked and helped doctors to save the lives of many thousands of people.

AMERICA

WAS NAMED AFTER AMERIGO VESPUCCI, A MERCHANT AND EXPLORER WHO SAILED TO THE MAINLAND SEVERAL YEARS AFTER COLUMBUS DISCOVERED THE NEW WORLD.

PLAYING WITH THE
YO-YO
WAS ONE OF THE FAVOURITE PASTIMES OF THE ANCIENT GREEKS

WHEN ST. PIERRE, MAJOR CITY OF MARTINIQUE, WAS WRECKED BY A VOLCANIC EXPLOSION ON MAY 8TH. 1908, ONLY AUGUSTE CIPARIS, IN JAIL FOR A MINOR OFFENCE, SURVIVED OUT OF THE 30,000 POPULATION.

THE RELIGION OF THE
TODAS
OF INDIA, FORBIDS THEM TO CROSS BRIDGES — THEY MUST ALWAYS FORD RIVERS.

FRAUD-OR WIZARD ?

Daniel Home, born in Scotland in 1833, grandson of the 10th Earl of Home, was one of the most controversial figures of the last century in spiritualist circles. He discovered his strange powers when he saw a chair in his room floating in mid-air, people heard spirit rappings whenever he was around and by the time he was 19, he was famous for his levitations. One time, he floated in the third floor window of his friend Lord Adare at Ashley House in London. Two other people in the room stepped back in horror as Home floated in horizontally and sat down in an easy chair. He appeared to be in a trance but when Lord Adare's brother-in-law said incredulously, "How on earth did he do it?", Home said, "I'll show you again", which he did by floating out of the window and back again. The three men claimed that in a trance he had also handled red hot coals without burning his hands.

At seances he held, he sat in a circle of nine people when spirit hands appeared, cold winds blew, perfumes wafted, bells rang and concertinas played. Heavy tables rose, apparently of their own accord. He himself rose from his chair and floated above his audience.

Famous conjurors and illusionists called him a fraud. Many tried to discredit him, diving under tables looking for wires, rubber gloves or any other device of trickery — none were ever found. Nobody ever proved trickery or found evidence of mass hypnotism and by the time he died at the age of 53 in 1886, people were calling him a wizard.

FLOWER GUARD

When Czar Nicholas I and his wife were strolling in the grounds of one of their country palaces, they spotted what appeared to be the first snowdrop of the year. When the Empress expressed a wish that it should not be picked, her husband ordered a soldier to stand guard over the tiny flower.

Some fifty years later, the Czar's great-grandson, Nicholas II was strolling in the same grounds when he spotted a lone sentry in the middle of the field. Puzzled by the presence of the sentry, he made inquiries and found that the order of Nicholas I had been entered in the guard log book and had never been counter-manded and a sentry had been dutifully posted on the same spot for half a century.

Yes Officer!

Constable, meaning police officer, comes originally from the Latin term "comes stabuli", which meant "Count of the Stable", he was the person who administered the household of an important personage.

FLY MOVE

Under the Roman government, a law in 43 BC ordered that the lands of the wealthy should be given up to war veterans, with the exception of cemeteries and mausoleums.

Virgil, the wealthy poet, who feared that his land on Esquiline Hill would soon be lost to him, sat and pondered how to get around the law.

He sent invitations to his friends for them to join him in a solemn ceremony. Senators gave mournful speeches and Virgil spoke tearfully of his sad loss as a tiny casket was buried on his land.

He was burying what he called his pet housefly and, although it cost him £50,000, the funeral effectively turned his land into a cemetery.

THE MAN-HATER

Sara Hyslop of Leigh, Edinburgh in Scotland, was proposed to 53 times in 10 years and left every one waiting at the alter after allowing each suitor to make all the arrangements. But number 54 turned the tables on Sarah and didn't turn up at the church. This so upset her that she gave up her career of jilting men and, in 1898, went to live in the South of France.

There she became known as a confirmed man-hater and would employ maids only if they took an oath to remain single.

She died at the age of 80 and 54 wedding dresses were found in her house. To each one was attached the photograph of the man who had proposed — with the eyes pierced by pins.

All in One Hour

In one hour you probably spoke 2,500 words, if you're allowed to, blinked 500 times and your heart pumped 2 tons of blood, and you lost enough body heat to boil 2 pints of water, your fingernails grew 327th of an inch.

Elsewhere, 12,000 more souls joined the human race — 2,000 of them Chinese, 2,000 couples were married, 1,300 couples were divorced. The earth travelled 66,000 miles in its orbit, 83 tons of cosmic dust fell to earth, it was shaken by 3 minor earthquakes and about 20 tremors. Lightning struck at least one person or building somewhere.

2,000 trans-Atlantic 'phone calls were made, ships sailed 6,000,000 miles, 'planes flew 11,000,000 miles and a snail managed to make 30 yards.

Some 30 New Yorkers were mugged and elsewhere 2 murders were committed and 100 robberies took place.

British housewives bought £635,000 worth of groceries, while the men spent £180,000 on booze and £17,000 on cigarettes.

What a busy lot we are.

Bible Story

The Old Testament contains 39 books, 929 chapters, 23,214 verses, 592,253 words and 2,738,100 letters.

The New Testament has 27 books, 270 chapters, 7,967 verses, 132,253 words and 933,380 letters.

In the Old Testament, the word Lord appears 1,853 times and Jehovah 5,845 times. The word "and" occurs 35,543 times and the word "reverend" only once.

The shortest verse in the Old Testament is I Chronicles i, 25; shortest in the New Testament is John xi, 35.

The ninth verse of the eighth chapter of Esther is the longest verse in the entire work.

How do we know all these curious facts about the Holy book?

Well, it's all thanks to the Prince of Granada, heir to the Spanish throne, who was for 33 years a prisoner in the Palace of Skulls, Madrid, with no companion except his Bible, which he faithfully perused each day and left his findings to posterity.

WILLY JUMPER

BOUNDING BILLY BARKER OF MANCHESTER HAD SUCH CONTROL OVER HIS BODY THAT HE COULD LEAP FROM A CANAL BANK, SINK HIS FEET JUST BELOW THE SURFACE OF THE WATER AND JUMP OUT ONTO THE OTHER SIDE WITHOUT HAVING TOUCHED THE BOTTOM. HE COULD ALSO PERFORM THIS FEAT BACKWARDS!

HE COULD JUMP OVER TWO CARTHORSES FROM A STANDING POSITION AND LEAP INTO A CRATE OF EGGS AND OUT AGAIN WITHOUT BREAKING ANY. HIS SECRET WAS TWO 25lb. WEIGHTS, ONE IN EACH HAND, WITH WHICH HE COULD CONTROL HIS IMPETUS, AND ALSO HIS SUPERB FITNESS.

HE DIED IN MARCH 1965 AGED 84.

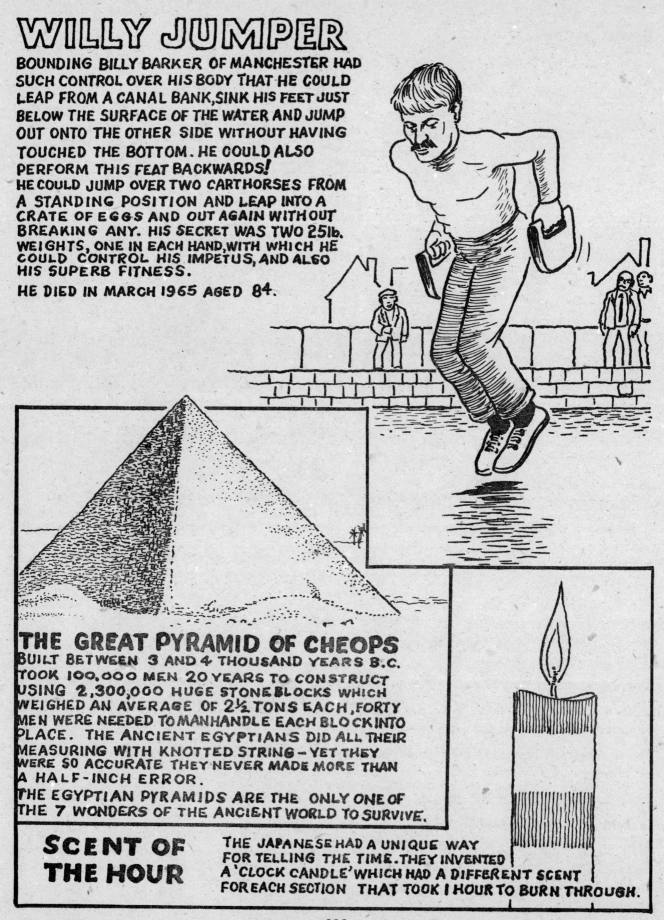

THE GREAT PYRAMID OF CHEOPS

BUILT BETWEEN 3 AND 4 THOUSAND YEARS B.C. TOOK 100,000 MEN 20 YEARS TO CONSTRUCT USING 2,300,000 HUGE STONE BLOCKS WHICH WEIGHED AN AVERAGE OF 2½ TONS EACH, FORTY MEN WERE NEEDED TO MANHANDLE EACH BLOCK INTO PLACE. THE ANCIENT EGYPTIANS DID ALL THEIR MEASURING WITH KNOTTED STRING — YET THEY WERE SO ACCURATE THEY NEVER MADE MORE THAN A HALF-INCH ERROR.

THE EGYPTIAN PYRAMIDS ARE THE ONLY ONE OF THE 7 WONDERS OF THE ANCIENT WORLD TO SURVIVE.

SCENT OF THE HOUR

THE JAPANESE HAD A UNIQUE WAY FOR TELLING THE TIME. THEY INVENTED A 'CLOCK CANDLE' WHICH HAD A DIFFERENT SCENT FOR EACH SECTION THAT TOOK 1 HOUR TO BURN THROUGH.

Grave Shock

Mourners ran screaming from the graveside of 56-year-old Antonio Percelli as he climbed, very much alive out of his coffin at Palermo, Sicily. But the shock killed his mother-in-law and she occupied the grave instead of him.

Golden Knockdown

Bill Stevenson, bored with knocking down buildings for a living, sold his demolition business in Memphis, Tennessee, and went to the Amazon to look for gold.

He found plenty of swamps, insects and reptiles . . . but not a sign of any gold.

Back home in the US, Bill, dissolusioned and nearly broke, bought an old farmhouse at Pilot Knob, Tennessee, with the intention of renovating it and selling it.

One day he was demolishing a wall with a pickaxe when suddenly a shower of coins poured out of the wall.

A local historian did some research and found that the treasure had been hidden in the wall by William Franklin, a colonel in the Civil War, who was killed in the 1860s. His secret had died with him.

Bill sold the coins for £25,000 — enough to set him up in the demolotion business again.

Old-Timers

Parrots are among the few creatures who rival humans for living to a good old age. Some have lived to more than 80 years old and one cockatoo reached the amazing age of 95.

Like humans these bird old-timers show signs of senility. They go bald and become forgetful, unable to remember the many words they once knew.

Dogs rarely reach more than 18 years. But one cross-bred terrier which died in 1956 was 23. Cats usually live for about 15 years but a Devonshire cat reached the grand old age of 35. Must be that Devonshire cream.

Another creature noted for totting up the years is the toad. One, in a zoo in Denmark, had 54 birthdays.

The tortoise, too, can survive some 60 years or more. So the pet that's ambling across the lawn may be older than you think, so let's have a little more respect for the old gentleman.

The little canary can reach 20 as can tame ravens and magpies.

In the insect world, Queen ants have been known to carry on for 15 years.

The TREACHEROUS SAND

The Culbin Sands

In the August of 1676, the Barony of Culbin was one of the most fertile and prosperous estates in Scotland. Situated in Morayshire, Culbin was ruled by the Laird of Kinnaird from his mansion. The estate held 16 farms.

One particular August evening the people of Culbin were in a happy mood celebrating another successful year and a heavy crop of barley nodding in the fields, awaiting the reaping next day. There was plenty of drinking and dancing and people scoffed at the old tinker when he prophesied that the crop would never be harvested.

That night the west wind gradually began to rise bringing a sprinkle of sand with it from the Culbin Sands. Suddenly the wind gathered in strength. The gentle rustling built up to a frightening shriek. Slowly the sand drifted up the sides of houses and buried the fat crops. Higher and higher the sand drifted, farmhouses disappeared and even the great manor house was submerged.

In a matter of days it was as if the estate had never existed. Most of the people escaped but 10,000 acres were buried under a weird sea of sand. In the middle there stands to this day, a huge dune called Lady Culbin. And underneath, it is believed, lies the buried manor house.

Perhaps one day another great west wind will come and blow away the treacherous sands of Culbin.

CHICKENS AND OTHERS

The Jacana Bird, found in India, Australasia and the tropical regions of America and Africa, has long legs and extraordinary long toes which enables it to walk on the floating leaves of water-lilies. It builds its nest which floats on the water.

Talking of nests, the Australian Bush Turkey doesn't believe in doing things by halves, it collects as much as 5 tons of twigs, leaves and other material to build its nest in which it lays its eggs to incubate.

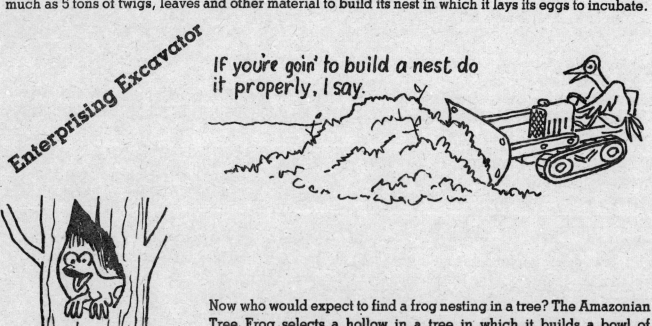

Now who would expect to find a frog nesting in a tree? The Amazonian Tree Frog selects a hollow in a tree in which it builds a bowl of waterproof beeswax. It obtains the beeswax from the comb of a friendly bee. Why the bees allow it to take the wax is a mystery. The bowl fills with rainwater in which the frog deposits its eggs. The little tadpoles feed off their tails until they're big enough to search for food outside the nest.

Chickens are descended from the jungle fowl of Asia. Some 5,000 years ago, man found it more convenient than hunting to keep animals and fowl around their living places — a handy supply of fresh food when required.

It's about time you were tamed and domesticated — its 3,000 B.C.

★

I'm bushed!

Egg — spanding Population!

no comment

Today there are about the same number of chickens in the world as people — four billion of them supply us with 400 billion eggs a year! The USSR has the biggest chicken population of any nation with 400 million of them.

★

Did you know the Giraffe is truly a "dumb" animal being unable to make any vocal sound? Also, in spite of its extra long neck, it only has the same number of bones in the neck as a mouse has, seven!

CHICKENS AND OTHERS

Another mammal that enjoys flitting from tree to tree is the chimpanzee, although a full grown chimp can weigh up to 12 stones, it is capable of supporting its weight on one finger when swinging from branch to branch.

Another tree dweller and expert trapezist is the Orang Utan found in Malaya, the name means "old man of the woods".

Globe Trotter

Now, not a tree dweller but a seabird which makes the longest nesting flight in the world, it actually travels from one end of the earth to the other. That is the Arctic Tern, which nests in the Arctic and then journeys 11,000 miles to spend winter in the Antarctic. It does this every year. Makes you wonder why!

The Steamer Duck of the Falklands stays put. It is unique in so far as it is able to fly when young but cannot do so in the adult stage. Maybe it's just too tired.

The Aardvark is probably known to many people because in a lot of dictionaries it is the first word to appear. The name comes from the Afrikaans and means "earth-pig". It has long ears, and sharp claws and a long, sticky tongue, and, although resembling a pig in some ways, it is a relative of the anteater. It uses its sharp claws to dig out ants nests and it can burrow faster than a man can dig with a spade. It is a nocturnal animal about 5 feet long and lives on ants and termites it catches with its sticky tongue. It lives in Africa.

? ? ? ?

Would you believe that . . .

The Owl has no movement in its eyes but to compensate for this it can revolve its head in an almost complete circle.

? ? ? ? ?

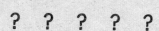

Pirate of the Skies

Still on seabirds, there is one that lives mainly by robbing other seabirds. It is the Frigate Bird which will "buzz" other birds carrying fish in their bills causing them to drop their catch. The robber then deftly catches its prize in mid-air.

CHICKENS AND OTHERS

Fly-weight

The Helenas humming bird, found in Cuba is so tiny that it often gets caught in spiders' webs. From tip to tail it is only 2¼ inches long, the body accounting for only half an inch of this. It weighs in at 1/18th of an ounce — the ostrich can tip the scales at 350 lbs, however it is a flightless bird.

The largest flying bird is the African Kori Bustard which can weigh as much as 40 lbs.

Hi, there, smallfry

Young at Heart

Falcons are the oldest inhabitants of the bird world, some are believed to have a life span of 150 years.

Why, I've lived in these 'yere parts egg and bird for 150 years, son.

In his case his bite is worse than his bark

The Barkless Dog

The Basenji, or Congo Bush Dog, which lives in the Congo basin in Western Africa, is unable to bark.

A chestnut and white dog, it grows to about 16 ins high. The most noise it can produce varies from a whimper to a laughing sound.

In the Pink

The long-legged pink Flamingo gets its lovely hue from the tiny shrimp-like water creatures that it eats. Deprived of this food, the bird's plumage turns white. It's the only bird that eats its food upside down, to do this it hangs its head and swishes the top part of its beak over the water and mud, bringing its food to the surface.

Living on lakesides in Africa, as they do in great colonies, they have solved the problem of flooding by building little mud towers in which they lay their eggs.

HI, POP!

See How They Fly

The Flying Squirrel doesn't really fly but glides, sometimes a hundred feet at a time, the only mammal that really flies with wings is the bat. The Flying Squirrel has flaps of skin between the front and back legs. To move from tree to tree the animal leaps in the direction it wants to go, opens its legs, stretching the skin flap as it does so and glides safely to its target. It's amazing the accuracy that it attains.

That's not flying, that's cheating

CHICKENS AND OTHERS

Desirable Residence —

The nest of the Australian Bower Bird is quite an artistic construction. It builds a kind of tunnel or bower of twigs and stiff grass. It then decorates its private playground with coloured pebbles, shells and flowers, etc.

Down-town Australia

...and this is early Australian.

Another well-known native of Australia is the kangaroo. There are several species, some measuring 5 feet in length of body with a tail over 4 feet long. The smallest is about the size of a rabbit. The kangaroo is not constructed to run but can bound along with its powerful hind legs at speeds of up to 40 mph in leaps of 15 to 20 feet. The longest kangaroo jump recorded was over 40 feet!

Fool! I nearly jumped out of my skin.

Boo!

What d'you mean, you're first up Everest?

High Flyers

Most birds don't fly above 3,000 feet but there are some notable exceptions. Geese flying in the Himalayas in Asia have been recorded as flying at 29,000 feet! A South American Condor once crashed into an aircraft at 20,000 feet.

Some Sprinter!

The fastest creature on four legs is the cheetah which has been known to top 70 mph when chasing its prey. A racehorse travels at 47 mph, ducks 70 mph. Ostriches can touch 50 mph on their strong two legs but tend to run in a wide circle.

Get along, slowcoaches!

But the well-named swift can leave them all behind, they can fly at 106 mph.

121

CHICKENS AND OTHERS

Red Alert!

Why is a bull irritated by the colour red? Well, it isn't because a bull is colour-blind, it doesn't see the colour but attacks a cape because it's being waved about.

Eye-Eye!

We always describe keen sight as being "eagle-eyed" and that's a pretty good description. The eagle has probably the best vision of all birds of prey, it has the ability to spot a rabbit from up to 2 miles away. Fish eagles can see fish swimming underwater from a great height and make a power dive on to their prey.

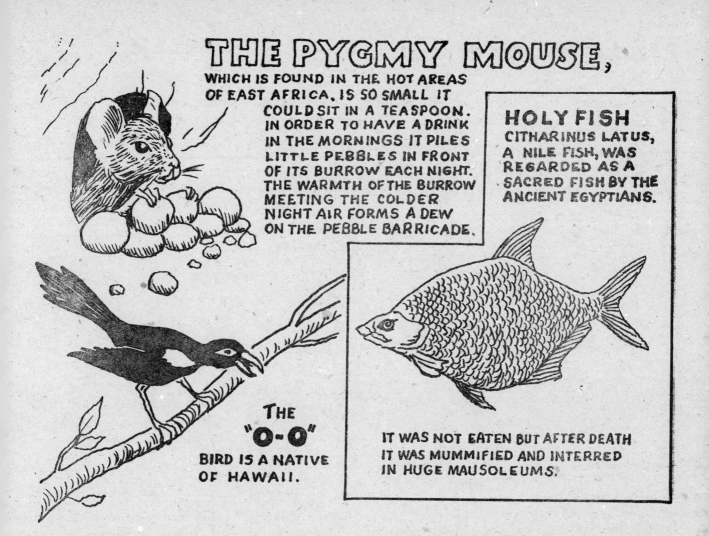

THE PYGMY MOUSE,

WHICH IS FOUND IN THE HOT AREAS OF EAST AFRICA, IS SO SMALL IT COULD SIT IN A TEASPOON. IN ORDER TO HAVE A DRINK IN THE MORNINGS IT PILES LITTLE PEBBLES IN FRONT OF ITS BURROW EACH NIGHT. THE WARMTH OF THE BURROW MEETING THE COLDER NIGHT AIR FORMS A DEW ON THE PEBBLE BARRICADE.

HOLY FISH

CITHARINUS LATUS, A NILE FISH, WAS REGARDED AS A SACRED FISH BY THE ANCIENT EGYPTIANS.

IT WAS NOT EATEN BUT AFTER DEATH IT WAS MUMMIFIED AND INTERRED IN HUGE MAUSOLEUMS.

THE "O-O" BIRD IS A NATIVE OF HAWAII.

HOW D'YOU DO?

INDIAN RULER KHAN JAHAN SO ENJOYED SHAKING HANDS WITH PEOPLE THAT WHEN HE DIED HE LEFT INSTRUCTIONS FOR HIS BODY TO BE BURIED IN A CONICAL TOMB - WITH HIS RIGHT HAND STUCK THROUGH THE WALL. EVERY VISITOR TO THE TOMB DUTIFULLY SHOOK HANDS WITH THE CORPSE UNTIL THE HAND WITHERED AWAY AFTER 40 YEARS.

Pearls, Pearls, Pearls

Pearls are usually associated with the exotic East and dusky skinned maidens diving in warm, south sea oceans, but did you know that there is a fortune in pearls lying on the beds of British rivers?

They just need finding. The only equipment needed is a knife, a bucket and a sharp eye to spot the freshwater mussel — oh yes, and infinite patience.

But that patience could be amply rewarded. The biggest and most valuable pearl found in a British river by Britain's only professional pearl fisherman, Bill Abernethy of Kincardineshire is a beautiful, glowing pink orb, ½ an inch in diameter and worth a cool £10,000. Smaller pearls can vary in price from five to one hundred and fifty pounds, depending on their quality.

Mussels are found only in clear, clean fast-flowing waters, they are allergic to dirty waters such as the Mersey, Clyde and the Thames. The best river is the Tay, but rivers all over Scotland, Wales in early Spring, Shropshire and Ireland also have a good yield.

The amateur pearl-fisherman should look for the oldest mussels with wrinkled or deformed shells — the pearls are formed in the same way as oyster pearls, by the creature forming protective layers of pearl around specks of grit that find their way into the inside of the shell.

British pearls are reputed to have a place in the Crown Jewels and even Julius Caesar had a breastplate studded with freshwater pearls.

* * * *

Talented Beasts

"Never work with children or animals" is an old showbiz maxim but a chap called Bisset put animals to work for him. He taught three cats to play the dulcimer (a stringed instrument struck with little hammers) and make a squawl in time to the music. They made him £1,000 in only a few days.

Later he taught canaries, linnets and sparrows to whistle in time, a hare to beat a drum, turkeys to dance and a tortoise to write names on the floor with its blackened feet.

He toured provincial fairs and was a great success with the 18th century crowds and made quite a business of it and also a fortune.

Rat Soup

The grim Dartmoor Prison, set in a barren, rocky waste at Princetown, whipped by rain and often shrouded in a blanket of clammy mist was once intended as a site for a village settlement

Sir Thomas Tyrwhitt actually built a few cottages and an inn there in 1771 but the climate doomed his chance of success.

Later the government added further buildings to Tyrwhitt's deserted settlement to house French prisoners of war.

In May, 1809, 2,500 prisoners moved in. They organised their own system of society in which "Lords", with plenty of money were the top, "Laboureurs", who made money by producing for sale, models and ornaments out of bones or any scraps they could find, and lastly "Romans", who would often gamble away their clothes and went about naked — a grim prospect in that climate. They were ruled by a tough man known as the "General".

The food was terrible. If rats fell into the soup cauldrons they were left in to give some "body" to the slop.

When some American prisoners were sent to the prison, the Frenchmen objected and riots broke out in which hundreds were injured.

At the end of the Napoleonic Wars the Frenchmen revolted at the delay in being returned to their homeland and British troops had to be called in. Although no shots were fired several prisoners died in bayonet charges.

In 1850, after the punishment of transportation for life to the colonies was abolished, Dartmoor was turned into a convict prison and the first 59 convicts were sent there. As new buildings were added the jail grew in importance but not in popularity

After over a century as a civil jail "The Granite Jug", as it was known to hundreds of ex-jailbirds, was closed for good.

SPY IN PETTICOATS

One of France's most successful 18th century spies had beautiful, flowing dark hair, a magnificent wardrobe of dresses and outfits, bracelets, necklaces and brooches.

She charmed her way into the highest circles of Europe where she extracted highly secret information from Kings and Emperors.

YET — THIS ENTRANCING SPY WAS A MAN!

This extraordinary ability to impersonate the opposite sex, brought the Chevalier D'Eon, when he was a young man, into contact with the King of France Louis.

His first spying assignment was to the court of Empress Elizabeth of Russia, his job was to talk her out of signing a treaty with Britain. Dressed as a woman, he was introduced to the Russian court as the "niece" of a fur trader.

The Empress was so delighted with the "charming French girl" that he became her close companion. It was then an easy task to persuade the ruler not to ally Russia to Britain.

Again, dressed as a woman, he arrived in London and managed to get hold of secret papers detailing England's coastal defences, he copied these and passed them to Paris.

Then, suddenly, D'Eon changed sides and asked for asylum in England, and informed the British Government of France's military plans.

After his defection, he often went secretly between London and Paris, working for the British. Several times he narrowly escaped capture, but each time his feminine dress and manners pulled him through.

In those days it was unthinkable that a male spy would wear frocks!

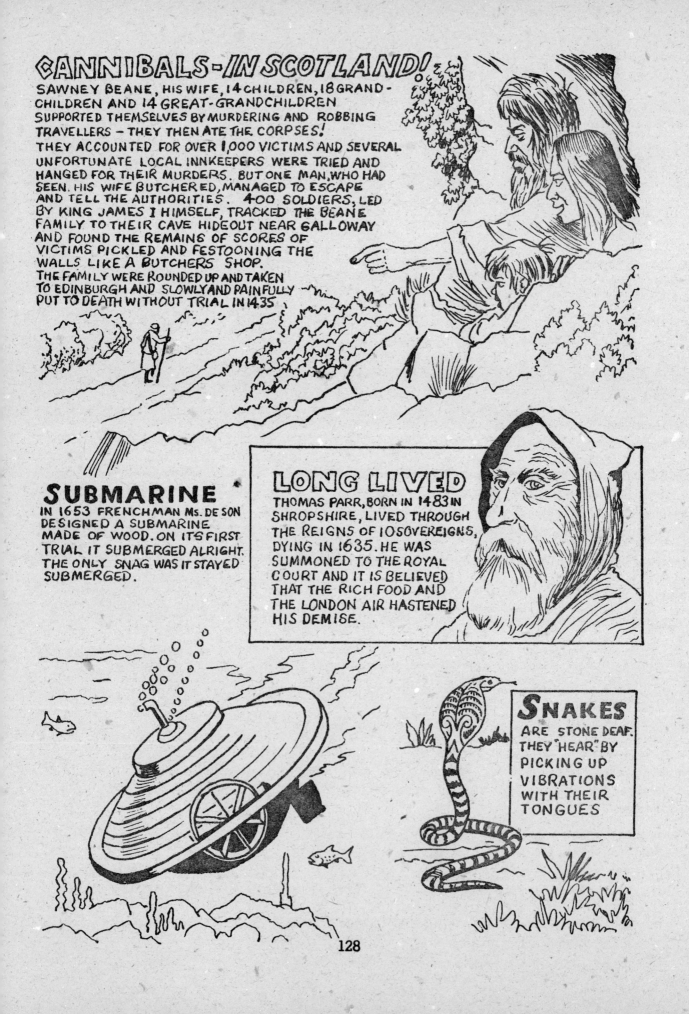

CANNIBALS — IN SCOTLAND!

SAWNEY BEANE, HIS WIFE, 14 CHILDREN, 18 GRAND-CHILDREN AND 14 GREAT-GRANDCHILDREN SUPPORTED THEMSELVES BY MURDERING AND ROBBING TRAVELLERS — THEY THEN ATE THE CORPSES!
THEY ACCOUNTED FOR OVER 1,000 VICTIMS AND SEVERAL UNFORTUNATE LOCAL INNKEEPERS WERE TRIED AND HANGED FOR THEIR MURDERS. BUT ONE MAN, WHO HAD SEEN HIS WIFE BUTCHERED, MANAGED TO ESCAPE AND TELL THE AUTHORITIES. 400 SOLDIERS, LED BY KING JAMES I HIMSELF, TRACKED THE BEANE FAMILY TO THEIR CAVE HIDEOUT NEAR GALLOWAY AND FOUND THE REMAINS OF SCORES OF VICTIMS PICKLED AND FESTOONING THE WALLS LIKE A BUTCHERS SHOP.
THE FAMILY WERE ROUNDED UP AND TAKEN TO EDINBURGH AND SLOWLY AND PAINFULLY PUT TO DEATH WITHOUT TRIAL IN 1435

SUBMARINE

IN 1653 FRENCHMAN Ms. DE SON DESIGNED A SUBMARINE MADE OF WOOD. ON ITS FIRST TRIAL IT SUBMERGED ALRIGHT. THE ONLY SNAG WAS IT STAYED SUBMERGED.

LONG LIVED

THOMAS PARR, BORN IN 1483 IN SHROPSHIRE, LIVED THROUGH THE REIGNS OF 10 SOVEREIGNS, DYING IN 1635. HE WAS SUMMONED TO THE ROYAL COURT AND IT IS BELIEVED THAT THE RICH FOOD AND THE LONDON AIR HASTENED HIS DEMISE.

SNAKES

ARE STONE DEAF. THEY "HEAR" BY PICKING UP VIBRATIONS WITH THEIR TONGUES

Soldiering On!

Sub-Lieutenant Hiroo Onoda, soldier of the Imperial Japanese army, received his orders, in 1944, from his commanding officer, Major Yoshimi Taniguchi, he was to stay put on Lubang Island in the Philippines and hold it for the glory of his Emperor.

He stayed alright — for 29 years after the war had officially finished and Japan defeated.

For years, police had trudged through the thick jungle on the island calling on him, through loudhailers, to surrender and stop shooting the local populace. That approach was always met with a volley of rifle-fire. In the last brush, Onoda's only remaining comrade was shot dead. Still he soldiered on, it was a disgrace for a Japanese to surrender to the enemy.

Even when photographs of the atom bomb attack on Hiroshima in 1945 were scattered all over the jungle in an attempt to persuade him that the war had really ended, only made Onoda more resolute, he had to obey his last order.

Then came the breakthrough. In 1974, a Japanese tourist came across the lieutenant, photographed him and chatted. He would only surrender, he said, to his commanding officer who had given him his last order.

So the ex-major was traced and flown out to Onoda's stronghold with a copy of Emperor Hirohito's 1945 order for all Japanese soldiers to lay down their arms and surrender to the Allied forces.

Finally convinced, Sub-Lieutenant Onoda — the man who had threatened his squad with death if they tried to desert — laid down his arms.

He was flown back to Tokyo for a re-union with his parents, who had believed him dead.

JACK KETCH – THE BUNGLING EXECUTIONER

The England of the 17th century was hardened to all sorts of brutality but even the people of those times were shocked by the monster that dominated the gallows scene for over 23 years, executioner Jack Ketch.

How Ketch managed to hold his job even in those cruel times is a mystery. He bungled every execution with an axe and during hangings would clown and caper about the scaffold until the hardest of crowds were revulsed. He often rifled the pockets of his victims and stripped off the clothes whilst the body was still twitching.

Ketch, pock-marked and dwarfish in stature, began his hideous career as public hangman in 1663, while still a young man. His first few years were passed dispatching minor highwaymen, petty thieves and the like and filling in with whippings, nose slitting, ear-cropping and branding, the usual punishment for minor offences.

His break into the "big-time" came in 1679 when he was chosen to execute the 30 people whose lives were sworn away by the treacherous villain, Titus Oates, with his false story of a Popish plot. Thrust into the public eye, Ketch strutted about the streets of London in bedraggled, ill-fitting finery, issued broadsheets such as the "Plotters Ballad, being Jack Ketch's incomparable receipt for the cure of traytorous diseases", illustrated with woodcuts showing Ketch waiting at Tyburn gallows saying "Here is your cure, sir" He hired swarms of urchings to hawk his ballad which became a "best seller" of the time.

The public outcry against Ketch's cruel bungling finally erupted over the execution of Lord William Russell in 1683, found guilty of plotting to kill the King and sentenced to be beheaded. After a short speech Lord Russell handed Ketch 10 guineas "to do his duty quickly", and placed his head upon the block. The squat executioner's first blow merely glanced off Lord Russell's shoulder who was heard to cry out "you dog, did I pay you ten guineas to use me so inhuman?" It took Ketch two more blows before the head was severed.

Ketch issued a broadsheet explaining his lack of skill as being due to Lord Russell fidgetting and also to being rudely interrupted by his assistant when taking aim.

In 1685 it was the Duke of Monmouth's turn to share the same fate as Lord Russell and, remembering the botch-up of that person's execution, handed Ketch 6 guineas and left a bag of gold with his servants to be given to his killer if he performed his task speedily and painlessly. The vile little man made an even bigger mess of his job, taking five blows to decapitate the luckless Duke. The crowd was so incensed that they demanded Ketch's person and he had to be escorted to safety by armed guards.

Throughout his career he squandered his earnings in tavern and bawdy house until in 1679, he was arrested for debt on his way back from "topping" three victims and paid his way out by selling the suits of his "clients".

Eventually he was thrown into prison for insulting a sheriff only to be released shortly after to execute his successor, a butcher by the name of Pascha Rose, who had committed murder. No one else but Ketch would take the job on.

However, he eventually finished up in debtors prison but once more he escaped and started a round of tavern visits with some cronies and finished up beating a poor gingerbread woman to death whilst he was completely intoxicated.

At his trial the vicious killer's defence was that he had a blackout and didn't know what was happening until he "came to". This plea of course, didn't save him from "dancing on air" as so many of his victims had done before him. He died in the November 1686.

Strangely enough, John Price, who was released from goal to hang Ketch, was himself executed for murder on the same gallows later.

THE DEMON DEACON

By day, Deacon William Brodie was a God-fearing, respectable councillor and churchgoer dressed in a fashionable suit. As night fell, the dark side of Brodie took over and a black suit and mask replaced the day clothes, and he led a gang of cut throats who indulged in wild orgies.

Whenever his trade of cabinet-maker took him into the house of a wealthy person, he made sure he got a wax impression of the front door key to be used some other night.

Things he spoke against during daily life as a churchman became part of his night life. He was to be found betting heavily on bloody cock fights, drinking heavily, lusting after women and robbing innocent townsfolk.

Then, each morning, he would sally forth in his respectable white suit acknowledging the smiles and greetings of people, some of whom he'd robbed the previous night. One time, when he broke into the home of a rich, elderly woman, he was recognised by her. However, he remained calm and walked to the table beside her and emptied the drawer of several hundreds of pounds, bowed to the woman and left.

The woman was so bemused that she thought she must have had an hallucination. The idea that the Deacon Brodie could be a thief was preposterous and she convinced herself that she had been seeing things.

But the truth dawned on her when Brodie was eventually betrayed by one of his gang and his double life was exposed.

Brodie was arrested and executed in 1788.

The Longest Wall in the World

Can you imagine a wall 1,500 miles long? This is the size of the longest wall in the world, the Great Wall of China. It was built in 221 BC by the Emperor Shi Huang Ti, to keep out China's enemies. It probably took 300,000 men ten years to complete as it had to be done completely by hand. It is constructed of brick, stone and earth and has watchtowers every tew hundred yards. It is as broad at its base as it is high, i.e. 25 feet. It tapers to a thickness of 15 feet at the top, where the workers paved a roadway.

Close Shave

For centuries man has removed the hair which sprouts daily on his face. Alexander ordered his army to be clean shaven but for a very practical reason. In hand-to-hand fighting it was found a beard gave a very good hand-grip to an enemy. Peter the Great, first Tsar of Russia, issued a law ordering his subjects to shave off — or have their beards pulled out by the roots. He later modified this by saying commoners could grow beards — if they paid a tax on them.

The early shaving blades were made of bronze and were about as sharp as a penknife, but shells, flintstone, a sliver of bamboo or even shark's teeth have been used to remove whiskers. In 1662, Samuel Pepys, the famous diarist, was using pumice stone to get a nice smooth face. But some two years later he recorded in his diary that he was using a more conventional razor and that, "It pleases me mightily". I should imagine it would after pumice stone.

The first safety-razor was invented in 1762, by Jean-Jacques Perret, a French master cutler. His cut-throat razor had a guard along one side of the blade which prevented it from slipping. Napoleon had a razor of silver-coated fine steel with a hand-carved ivory handle.

But the break-through to the modern razor familiar today, was made by the oddly-named American, King Camp Gillette, in the last century. He came up with the idea of a cheap, disposable blade.

13 -
LUCKY FOR SOME!

THIRTEEN, CONSIDERED TO BE UNLUCKY BY MANY, ONCE SAVED A SOLDIER'S LIFE. DURING THE REIGN OF WILLIAM III, PRIVATE JOHN HATFIELD WAS ACCUSED OF BEING ASLEEP ON GUARD DUTY AT WINDSOR PALACE ~ A CHARGE THAT CARRIED THE DEATH PENALTY. HATFIELD'S ONLY DEFENCE WAS THAT HE COULDN'T HAVE BEEN ASLEEP BECAUSE HE'D HEARD GREAT TOM, THE BELL IN THE CLOCK TOWER OF WESTMINSTER PALACE, STRIKE 13 TIMES AT MIDNIGHT. THE FACT THAT GREAT TOM WAS 20 MILES AWAY ONLY SERVED TO CONVINCE THE COURT OF HIS GUILT AND HE WAS SENTENCED TO DEATH.

HOWEVER, WHILST HE WAS IN THE DEATH CELL AWAITING EXECUTION, SEVERAL WITNESSES CAME FORWARD AND VERIFIED THAT THE CLOCK HAD INDEED STRUCK THIRTEEN THAT MIDNIGHT. HATFIELD RECEIVED THE ROYAL PARDON.

NOT A CLANG!

THE LARGEST BELL EVER CAST HAS NEVER BEEN HUNG OR RUNG. WEIGHING 198 TONS, MORE THAN 60 FT. ROUND THE RIM AND 19 FT. HIGH. IT HAS STOOD ON A PEDESTAL NEAR THE KREMLIN IN MOSCOW SINCE 1836.
IT WAS CRACKED IN THE FOUNDRY

EDWARD VI (1547-53) SON OF HENRY VIII AND JANE SEYMOUR, SUCCEEDED HIS FATHER TO THE THRONE AT THE AGE OF NINE. HE DIED OF CONSUMPTION IN 1553

HIPPOPOTAMUS
ACTUALLY MEANS 'RIVER HORSE'

ALTHOUGH CLUMSY AND UNGAINLY ON LAND THESE ANIMALS ARE EXTREMELY AGILE IN WATER. THEY CAN ACTUALLY RUN ALONG THE BED OF A RIVER.

The SAMURAI SWORD

Long recognised as the greatest sword makers in the world, the Japanese inscribed a "guarantee" of performance on each blade, for instance, "one body cut in the second position", meant a clean cut through the upper chest. The Samurai warriors, for whom the swords were mainly made, wanted, and got, the finest blades possible.

How were the blades tested then? The makers had one simple method of testing their products, they bought condemned prisoners from the local jail and sliced them in half. Sometimes two or three were cut through with one blow, this was duly recorded on the blade along with the signature of the maker.

They were also given names like "Monster Cutter" and "Dew on the Grass", the latter because of the shiny spots of super hard steel which gave the blade its tremendous cutting edge, it also carried the signature of its maker, 14th. Century swordsmith Shidzu Saburo Kaneuji, inlaid in gold. In recent times this sword was sold for £37,780.

These Samurai swords were believed to have a life of their own and were passed from father to son and were regarded as their most precious possessions, once drawn they had to kill — or the owner would be killed himself. A Samurai duel was to the death and after circling round each other for minutes on end, swords were drawn and used in seconds, leaving the loser on the ground — probably chopped in two.

Dr W. Compton, an American sword collector, found one that had been brought back as a souvenir and turned out to be a Japanese national treasure, and when he returned it he was decorated with the Order of the Rising Sun, so highly was the sword regarded

LENTINI, 3-LEGGED WONDER-MAN

The doctor and the child's mother had to rescue her newborn son from under the bedclothes where the midwife had tried to hide him. The reason was obvious, Frank Lentini had been born with an almost full-sized third leg growing from the right side.

Doctors told his mother that the reason for the extra limb was part of an undeveloped twin which was attached to the spine and could not be removed for danger of paralysis or death.

When he was eight, in 1907, the family (he had seven sisters and four brothers, all normally formed), left their home in Sicily to live in America.

Tempting offers from circuses were made to the Lentinis for their three-legged son to tour with them. But they steadfastly turned down all offers in order to allow their son to live as normal a life as possible.

His schoolfellows poked fun at Frank and he became very depressed until his parents took him to a home for handicapped children. Seeing the crippled and deformed youngsters, many much more deformed than he made him determined to make the best he could of life. "From that time I never complained. I think life is beautiful and I enjoy living it," he said later

He became a good scholar and could speak four languages by the time he left school, it was then that he decided to accept one of the circus offers.

He found the financial rewards were good and he learned to ride bicycles and horses and also played three-legged football which proved to be very popular with the public. Special three legged suits were made for him and he always had to buy two pairs of shoes but he gave the spare shoe to a one legged friend. Lentini married and had four normal children and lived to the age of 67, still working in the circus until his death in 1966.

INTO THE VALLEY OF DEATH

The struggle between Britain, France and Turkey with Russia was at its height when probably the best known, but suicidal, cavalry charge took place.

The blunder occurred when the commander of the British forces, Lord Raglan saw that the Russians were removing guns they had captured from the Turks. In a hastily scribbled note Raglan gave the order, "The heavy and light cavalry will advance rapidly and try to prevent the enemy from carrying away the guns." Captain Edward Nolan was given the job of delivering the note to Lord Lucan, the cavalry commander. When Nolan gave the note he was asked, "Attack what guns?", but Nolan instead of explaining about the Turkish guns waved vaguely towards the mouth of the valley, a valley bristling with Russian guns.

Although the Russians removing the Turkish guns were quite visible to Raglan on a 600 ft high ridge above the valley, they were out of sight of the cavalry.

Lord Lucan could only see the Russian guns so he ordered the attack on them. The charge was blown and Lord Cardigan, in charge of the Light Brigade, shouted: "The brigade will advance, the first squadron of the 17th Lancers directing."

As they trotted into the mouth of the valley, Cardigan and his lancers could see that death awaited them, but Cardigan never hesitated, drawing his sword he spurred his horse onward followed by the men of the Light Brigade, full of respect for their leader's courage and a fear of his strict discipline, the 673 officers and men, swords and lances at the ready, galloped towards the muzzles of the Russian artillery.

The Russian gunners held their fire until the quickly advancing cavalry were halfway along. Then they fired. With one tremendous blast the guns cut down a hundred riders and horses like a giant scythe. Amongst them, Captain Nolan, desperately trying to reach Cardigan to tell him of the mistake that had been made.

Brandishing his sword Cardigan roared above the cannon fire: "Steady the 17th Lancers." Onward they charged towards the guns at the head of the valley. At a range of 80 yards the guns opened fire — blasting the first of the riders to bits.

Lord Cardigan's horse was blown sideways but he quickly pulled his horse's head round and charged straight into the centre of the firing, being the first to reach the guns. The remainder of the Lancers leapt forward over the bodies of their comrades and engaged in hand-to-hand fighting with the gunners.

Meanwhile, Cardigan was making his way back through the carnage that was the Light Brigade. He said later, "It is not the duty of a general to join his soldiers in hand-to-hand fighting."

The Light Brigade gathered for another attack in order to hack out an escape route. But the Russians withdrew and the survivors walked wearily back to the British lines, leading their tired mounts. There was no fire from the guns on the sides of the valley — a French force of 300 had mopped up the gunners with little loss. In the 20 minutes it had taken to charge and retire, 247 of the 673 officers and men had been killed or wounded.

A French general, who watched the charge from a ridge, said: "It is magnificent, but it is not war. It is madness."

WHERE DID THEY GO ?

The mystery of the "Marie Celeste" has puzzled people for years but other less publicised events have occurred that have had no explanation to this day, and probably never will.

For instance, how does any army of 4,000 well-equipped, seasoned troops vanish into thin air? This is apparently what happened during the Spanish War of Succession, 1702–1714.

The troops, having camped overnight in the foothills of the Pyrenees, broke camp and continued on their march and were never seen again. There was no sign of a battle, no trace of scattered equipment, no bodies, nothing. To this day nobody knows what happened to them.

A little nearer our time is the mystery of what became of the two man crew of a De Haviland light bomber on desert patrol in Egypt in 1924. When the aircraft, which carried no radio, became an hour overdue back at its base airfield, routine rescue search operation was begun.

Within a short time, the missing aircraft was spotted on the ground and a land detail was directed to it. The men of the detail found the 'plane in perfect order, the motor started when the propeller was swung, there were no bullet holes or any other signs of damage, the only thing missing was the crew. The only trace of them were two sets of footprints in the sand leading away from the machine. The tracks were clear and well defined for fifty yards and then they stopped abruptly. It was as if the two airmen had stepped into another dimension — perhaps they had, who knows? The area for miles around was searched thoroughly but not a footprint or any other evidence was found of the two men; they had literally vanished from the face of the earth never to be seen again.

It is not only the military that has suffered mysterious disappearances, of course. Farmer Lang of Gallatin, Tennessee, USA, vanished into thin air before the eyes of several witnesses on the afternoon of the 23rd September, 1880. The facts are well documented and authenticated. As he left his home, his two children, Sarah aged 11 and David aged 8, were playing at the front of the house. A local judge, Augustus Peek, and a friend were driving by in their horse and trap. The pair called out to Lang, who waved to them and started walking across the field towards them, then vanished.

The judge and his friend, completely astounded, pulled up. They dismounted and ran towards the spot they had last seen the farmer, but he had simply disappeared. There were no holes or pits he could have fallen into, the land was completely flat and unmarked. There was just no accounting for his disappearance. Strangely enough, a wide circle of grass around the spot where Lang was last seen, took on a different colour over the next twelve months. His children said that they had heard their father's voice calling for help and growing fainter as time passed. No explanation has ever been given for the mystery, nor ever will be.

During the last war, in 1944, when the Japanese were being driven out of the Pacific, six US Helldiver Bombers, each with a crew of three, set out on a routine sweep of their sector in the hope of finding the odd enemy ship or submarine running for their home port. An hour after take-off, the airfield received a call for help from the patrol leader because the compasses in each 'plane were going haywire. A course was radioed but the patrol found it impossible to follow because of the behaviour of their compass needles. After more frantic calls, a huge flying boat with a thirteen man crew, including two navigators, was sent to guide the formation back to base, but it too had to send emergency calls for help when it reached the Helldivers' position; all four compasses on the flying boat were acting in the same erratic way. Then came silence.

Six heavily armed 'planes and the flying boat had just vanished. There were no enemy aircraft for hundreds of miles and no mention was made in the radio messages of any enemy ships or activity in the area. No wreckage or survivors were ever found although extensive sea searches were made in the area.

Who can say where all these men and machines went to? It still remains a mystery.

? ? ? ? ? ? ? ?

A NOSE FOR TROUBLE

CYRANO DE BERGERAC, 17th CENTURY POET, WIT AND EXPERT SWORDSMAN FOUGHT AND WON **1,000** DUELS OVER INSULTS ABOUT HIS OVER-SIZE CONK, SORRY, I MEAN NOSE DURING ONE 3 MONTH PERIOD HE 'RAN THROUGH' FOUR PEOPLE EACH WEEK.

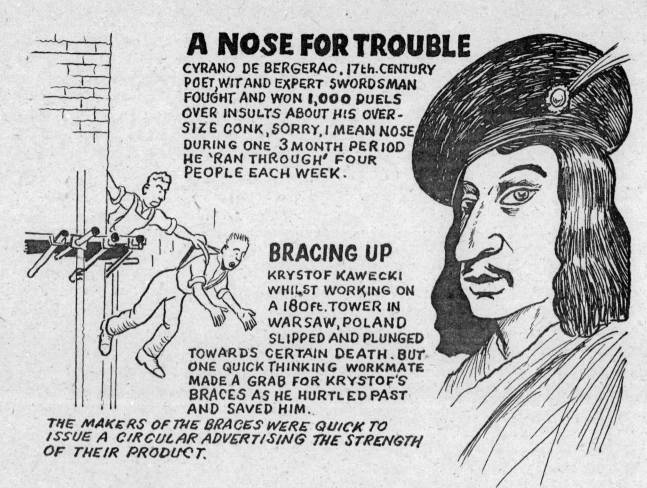

BRACING UP

KRYSTOF KAWECKI WHILST WORKING ON A 180ft. TOWER IN WARSAW, POLAND SLIPPED AND PLUNGED TOWARDS CERTAIN DEATH. BUT ONE QUICK THINKING WORKMATE MADE A GRAB FOR KRYSTOF'S BRACES AS HE HURTLED PAST AND SAVED HIM.

THE MAKERS OF THE BRACES WERE QUICK TO ISSUE A CIRCULAR ADVERTISING THE STRENGTH OF THEIR PRODUCT.

TOP CHAPEAU

£14,032 WAS THE PRICE PAID BY A FRENCH CHAMPAGNE FIRM IN APRIL 1970 FOR **ONE** HAT. IT WAS THE FAMOUS ONE WHICH BELONGED TO THE EMPEROR NAPOLEON.

DEAD BUT HE WOULDN'T LIE DOWN

KING LOUIS IX OF FRANCE "DIED" OF THE PLAGUE AT THE AGE OF 29 IN 1244.

BUT THE KING HAD OTHER IDEAS FOR, TO EVERYONE'S HORROR, DURING HIS FUNERAL SERVICE HE SAT UP IN HIS COFFIN.

HE LIVED FOR ANOTHER 26 YEARS, FOUGHT A CRUSADE AND WAS EVENTUALLY DECLARED A SAINT.

MYSTERY OF THE HUMAN TORCHES

No-one knows why some people burst into flames, the scientific phrase is "spontaneous combustion in human beings", but it has been happening for thousands of years, in biblical times it was called "Fire from Heaven" or "A Visitation from God", whatever it may be called, it is one of nature's greatest unexplained mysteries. When it does occur, the cause of death is recorded as "unknown".

Take these actual cases, usually fire is confined to the victim whilst the surroundings remain untouched.

22-year-old Phyllis Newcombe was happily dancing in a dance hall in 1938 when, in an instant, she was enveloped in flames before several hundred people and burned to death. The coroner decided that the woman's dress had been set alight by a cigarette.

In the summer of 1938, Mrs Carpenter was enjoying a holiday with her family, boating on the Norfolk Broads, when she was enveloped by flames and was soon reduced to ashes before the eyes of her horrified family. The family and the boat were completely untouched.

In 1943, Madge Knight burned to death in her bed in her Sussex home, yet the bedclothes were not even scorched.

In the case of Mrs Reeser of St Petersburg, USA, who spontaneously burned to death in 1957, the easy chair in which she was sitting became a pile of ash and metal springs, yet police, soon on the scene, found her skull reduced to the size of an orange and one foot that had been untouched in a slipper.

In April 1970, an 89-year-old widow, Margaret Hogan, was found burned to death whilst sitting in her favourite armchair in her Dublin home. Although Mrs Hogan's body was reduced to ashes, the chair was not badly burned and the linoleum beneath was only slightly charred.

Another widow, Euphemia Johnson, 68, of Sydenham, London, was consumed by flames in 1922, but her clothes and room were completely undamaged.

In 1939, 11-month-old Peter Seaton, of London, was in bed when a visitor to the house rushed to his room alarmed by the boy's screams. When he opened the door he was met by a searing blast of heat. The youngster died in the flames — yet the room was hardly damaged.

It seems incredible that a human body can burst into flames without actually being set alight and continue to burn without more fuel to keep it burning. Stranger still, it seems that the phenomenon is not confined to living people, for there was the corpse of a Mrs Satlow that was consumed by fire whilst in a coffin in a locked mortuary.

These unexplained conflagrations are but a few of the many that have occurred, and, stranger still, why such intense heat that can reduce a body to ashes, rarely damages the surroundings.

SIMEON THE STYLITE -
LIVED FOR 37 YEARS ON TOP OF A PILLAR!

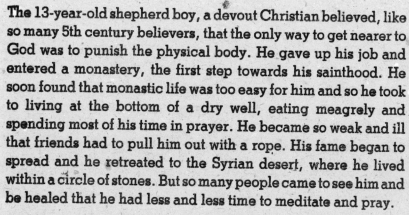

The 13-year-old shepherd boy, a devout Christian believed, like so many 5th century believers, that the only way to get nearer to God was to punish the physical body. He gave up his job and entered a monastery, the first step towards his sainthood. He soon found that monastic life was too easy for him and so he took to living at the bottom of a dry well, eating meagrely and spending most of his time in prayer. He became so weak and ill that friends had to pull him out with a rope. His fame began to spread and he retreated to the Syrian desert, where he lived within a circle of stones. But so many people came to see him and be healed that he had less and less time to meditate and pray.

His next move was to the top of a sixty foot high pillar situated thirty miles from Antioch in the midst of a sun-scorched wilderness. He remained there for the next 37 years in every extreme of weather, praying and posturing or standing with arms outstretched in the form of a cross for as long as eight hours at a time.

Other times he would bow repeatedly, his head almost touching his feet. He was once seen to repeat this gesture 1,240 times before collapsing on his yard wide platform.

Crowds of pilgrims and worshippers came from many miles around to pray with Simeon, disciples kept him fed by placing food and water in the basket lowered by the saint.

It was on the morning of January 5th, 459, Simeon failed to greet the rising sun. He was dead, still atop his pillar, without doubt his great feat of endurance helped to spread Christianity throughout the Roman Empire.

The stump of Simeon's pillar still remains.

IN THE EIGHT YEARS BETWEEN 1601-1609 2,000 NOBLE FRENCHMEN DIED IN DUELS

THE GENERAL WAS A LADY!

"JAMES" BARRY SERVED IN THE BRITISH ARMY FOR 52 YEARS — WITHOUT HER FELLOW OFFICERS REALISING THAT "HE" WAS A WOMAN.
AS A RESULT OF AN UNFORTUNATE LOVE AFFAIR SHE POSED AS A MAN AND JOINED THE ARMY IN 1813 RISING TO THE RANK OF GENERAL IN THE MEDICAL CORPS. SHE WAS DESCRIBED AS A "WAYWARD MAN WITH A QUARRELSOME TEMPER, A SUCCESSFUL DUELIST AND A SKILLFUL PHYSICIAN."
IT WAS NOT UNTIL HER DEATH IN 1865 THAT HER TRUE SEX WAS DISCOVERED — NOT EVEN THE SERVANT WHO HAD BEEN WITH HER FOR 50 YEARS SUSPECTED HER SECRET.

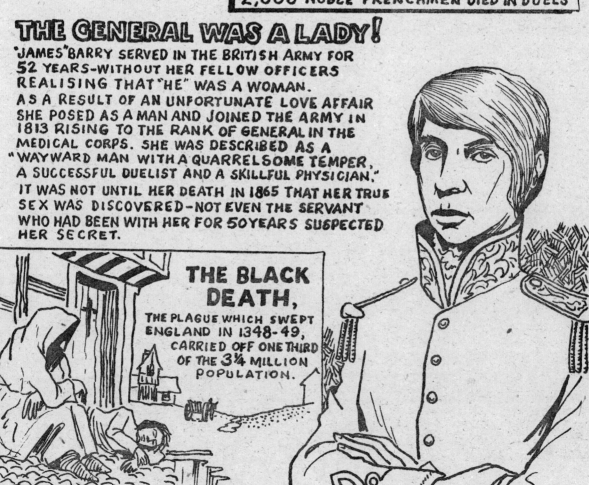

THE BLACK DEATH, THE PLAGUE WHICH SWEPT ENGLAND IN 1348-49, CARRIED OFF ONE THIRD OF THE 3¼ MILLION POPULATION.

FAMILY BUTCHER

During the 1920's, meat was scarce and very expensive in Berlin, so when Karl Denke, a butcher, began to sell tasty but inexpensive smoked pork, customers flocked to his shop door, he was rarely without a queue. Though they were puzzled by his moderate prices, they asked no questions, presuming that Denke had a direct supplier in the country.

But when Denke became involved in a shouting argument with a neighbour, local police came around to investigate and, during their inquiries, they searched his shop premises. What a shock they had, for at the back of the shop, were several barrels of freshly smoked, not pork, but human flesh. There were also boxfuls of human bones and lard rendered from the carcasses of Denke's 52 murder victims.

A ledger was also found, beautifully kept and recording the date of each murder and the weight of the body.

There must have been some very queasy stomachs around the area after that.

MILLIONS TO ONE CHANCES

The plane carrying Captain Hedley as an observer over the German lines on January 6th, 1918, was attacked and forced into an almost vertical dive — throwing Hedley out in mid-air minus a parachute.

After falling for several hundred feet the captain landed astride the fuselage of the aircraft he'd just left! The plane flew back to base and landed safely.

Another episode in the first World War involved a German sniper and a British soldier, both intent on killing each other. The German sighted and fired just as the British soldier got his foe in his sights, the German's bullet actually went down the barrel of his opponent's rifle, exploding a cartridge in the breech but causing no harm to the man — a million to one chance.

Yet another coincidence with a firearm, but one with tragic consequences, was when an American policeman, cleaning his gun in his house, dropped the weapon and a bullet accidentally left in the chamber, fired. The bullet splintered through the front door, travelled 138 feet into a crowd of children and killed the policeman's 7 year old daughter! A truly tragic stroke of fate.

The next amazing story concerns the aircraft that shot itself down! It happened when the pilot of a US navy jet, on a practice flight in 1956, fired a burst of dummy cannon shells and then went into a steep dive. The jet developed a speed greater than the falling shells and actually flew into a shower of them, which shattered his canopy and forced him to make an emergency landing.

The sea also has its share of amazing coincidences, such as when, on May 10th 1887, the sailing ship, Northumberland was wrecked in a terrible storm off the port of Napier, New Zealand. Dismasted and battered she sank to the bottom of the sea. The owners of the ill-fated ship sold out to another concern which retained the old firm's flags and ship's names. The time moves on to February 3rd 1931, and the steamship Northumberland was in Napier harbour when the port was rocked by an earthquake which caused the headland to shift into the sea raising the sea-bed by almost 20 feet. Right alongside the steamship which had inherited its name, rose the barnacle encrusted hulk of the sailing ship Northumberland, almost 44 years after her wrecking. Again, a chance in a million.

And now a 1 to 635,013,559,600 chance, this time with cards and again in New Zealand and not once but twice in consecutive deals. In 1939 in Christchurch, an old pack of cards, shuffled, then dealt to 4 people, gave each player perfect suits. This should happen only once in 44 million years yet in the next deal with a new pack each player was dealt 8 cards of one suit and 5 of another. A phenomenal happening.

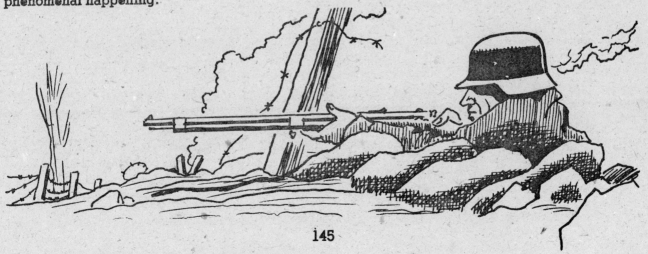

The AMAZING MONKS

The British Royal Engineers Officer, forcing his way through a blizzard in the Himalayas, thought at first that the weather was playing tricks with his imagination when he saw the figure of an almost naked monk sitting in the snow, deep in meditation.

But it was no hallucination, for on closer inspection, the officer saw that the man was indeed flesh and blood and, remarkably, the snow was actually melting as it came into contact with the man's naked flesh!

Other witnesses of this extraordinary feat, the resistance of the physical body to extremes of cold or hot, describe how these holy men will sit in freezing temperatures by the side of a mountain stream whilst an attendant drapes soaking wet blankets on the naked body of the monk, who will dry blanket after blanket purely from the heat generated from within his body.

It is certainly not a trick, but part of the religious training undertaken by these "tsampas", students of mind over matter. The cold and heat resistance is only a minor accomplishment and is merely a demonstration of the obedience of the body to the mind.

One of the stages the disciples have to go through is to be shut away from the outside world in complete darkness with nothing but barley, roots and water pushed into their cells each day for food. There they remain for 3 years, 3 months and 3 days, during which time the only contact they have is with their "guru" or teacher, by telepathy, mind communication.

Once it is mastered, "tummo" as it is known, enables the mind to work all manner of wonders, to create ghosts of people, perform levitation, that is to raise the body above the ground, defying the law of gravity. It can also be used to create objects, by thought concentration. A "phurba" or magic dagger was once made to appear in the hand of a hostile king called Langdharma and cut his throat, after which it was made to vanish.

The main purpose of all the exercises and training is purely religious and a supreme effort to understand the Almighty God.

≪ ≪ ≪ ≪ ≪ ≪ ≫ ≫ ≫ ≫ ≫ ≫

NEW-BORN BABY WEIGHS IN AT 2½ TONS

The blue whale, the largest animal ever known to inhabit the earth, gives birth to a baby 25 ft in length and about 2½ tons in weight.

In the ten and three-quarter months before and twelve months after the young is born, it grows from a tiny egg, weighing a fraction of a milligramme, to twelve or fifteen tons. The most rapid growth in the animal world.

A full grown whale has been known to weigh one hundred and seventy tons.

The DISCERNING GUN

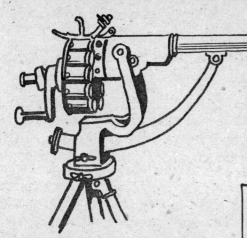

THIS SURPRISINGLY MODERN LOOKING WEAPON IS A VERY EARLY FORM OF MACHINE-GUN. INVENTED IN 1718 BY AN ENGLISHMAN, JAMES PUCKLE, IT COULD BE FIRED "63 TIMES IN 7 MINUTES BY ONE MAN EVEN IN THE RAIN" THE AMAZING THING IS IT COULD FIRE ROUND BULLETS AT CHRISTIANS AND SQUARE ONES AT INFIDELS. IT WAS NOT TAKEN UP BY THE GOVERNMENT.

PUP IN A CUP

BRED IN WESTERN GERMANY, A MINIATURE YORKSHIRE TERRIER IS SO TINY IT CAN SIT IN A TEACUP! BUT THEY'RE WORTH OVER £1,000 EACH - £100 AN OUNCE.

THE GREAT BLUE WHALE

IS THE LARGEST LIVING CREATURE THAT HAS EVER EXISTED, WEIGHING ABOUT THREE TIMES AS MUCH AS THE LARGEST DINOSAUR.

LUNG POWER

THE NATIVES OF THE ISLAND OF GOMERA, OFF THE COAST OF NORTH AFRICA, COMMUNICATE WITH EACH OTHER OVER A DISTANCE OF 3 OR 4 MILES WITH A SYSTEM OF WHISTLED CODES.

The Kennedy—Lincoln Coincidence

Kennedy was elected in 1960

Kennedy's secretary was named Lincoln

Lincoln was elected in 1860

Lincoln's secretary's name was Kennedy

Both secretaries advised their presidents not to go to the places where they were assassinated. Both men were shot in the presence of their wives.

The successor of each president was named Johnson — Andrew Johnson, born 1808 — Lyndon Johnson, born 1909.

Of the two assassins, Booth was born in 1839, Oswald was born in 1939. Both men were killed before they could be tried.

Both presidents were deeply concerned with the Civil Rights problem of their particular time.

Lincoln and Kennedy were carried to their graves on the same caisson.

VLAD THE IMPALER

"Vlad the Impaler" was the name earned by Vlad, King of Rumania in 1456 because of the terrible method of execution he favoured. One January morning in 1461, Turkish prisoners were hurled one by one into a valley, the floor of which bristled with thousands of spears, points upwards, skewering the screaming Turks who were left to die in agony. Three thousand men were impaled before the King sat down to his breakfast.

Vlad succeeded his weak father in 1456, and immediately set about ridding the country of the bandits which infested it. Then, with a force of chosen bodyguards, he went from town to town, putting on trial corrupt officials — the penalty, of course, was impaling. Over five hundred met their deaths in this manner. When several powerful landowners protested at this cruelty, Vlad invited them to a banquet in his castle — a feast prepared with sharp stones mixed in — and, when his guests complained, he accused them of slighting his hospitality and promptly impaled them, their families and servants.

Vlad then went against Turkey, which had Rumania in its power at the time, by refusing to pay the yearly taxes imposed by the Turks and to stop sending the five hundred men required each year by the Turkish Army. It wasn't very long before Turkish envoys arrived, demanding an explanation. Vlad ordered them to remove their turbans in his presence; they, of course, refused saying that it was against their religion. The bodies of the envoys were sent to the sultan with the turbans nailed to their heads!

Whilst awaiting the expected attack from the Turks, King Vlad terrorised his own subjects in order to make them more afraid of him than the enemy. A total of twenty thousand men and women were impaled and it became the standard punishment for almost every offence.

Vlad eventually met his fate when thirty thousand of the Sultan's soldiers trapped and slaughtered him in his own palace. The Rumanians rejoiced more than the Turks at the tyrant's death. In fact, to this day, Vlad's defeat is recorded in Rumanian history books as the people's happiest victory.

? ? ? ? ? ? ? ? ? ? ? ? ? ? ? ? ? ? ?

Count St Germain

WHERE HE CAME FROM NO-ONE KNOWS...

Count St Germain was one of the most mysterious figures to be found in history. Although he appeared very rich his tastes were very simple, he didn't touch alcohol and was a vegetarian, but nobody ever knew the source of his wealth.

The earliest known appearance was in 1710 when he was described as being 45 or 50 years old and a witty and brilliant conversationalist, his knowledge of precious stones, of which he owned many, was first class. In 1743 he attended the court of Louis XV and, although a complete stranger, made a most favourable impression. He spoke several European and eastern languages, Latin, Ancient Greek and Arabic, he was an expert in physics and chemistry, inventing new ways of curing leather and dying cloth and could also turn iron into a metal resembling gold.

He involved himself in various scientific and political activities and yet still found time to travel about Europe and to visit India, Persia, North Africa and Russia, his travels took him to every major court in Western Europe.

It so happened that in the late 1750's he came across some people who had known him in 1710, and they found him looking as young as he did when they first met him 40 years previously. By the 1770's he was thought to be about 60 but remaining vigorous and still travelling widely.

His death was reported in 1784 yet a year later some old friends of his saw him in Wilhelmsbad, Germany, attending a conference of occult groups. Shortly before the French Revolution he turned up at Versailles to warn the king, Louis XVI, about the gathering storm of unrest about to explode in France. 1789 saw him at the Court of the King of Sweden on political business. Then St Germain seemed to vanish for all time until a Madame d'Adhemar claimed that he had visited her in 1820, this would have made him about 150 years old! But that was the last anyone ever saw of him, he just disappeared as mysteriously as he first appeared.

THE MAD KING CHRISTOPHE OF HAITI

Christophe, the power-crazy ruler of Haiti, to demonstrate the loyalty of his guards, paraded them before his castle and then ordered them to march over a 200 ft high cliff. Those who obeyed plunged to their death, those who didn't were horribly mutilated before being executed.

His stronghold, built in 1807, shortly after coming to power stood on a mountain several thousand feet high. Every piece of building material, half-a-million tons of it, had to be manhandled up the mountainside and 20,000 men died of strain and exhaustion before the castle was completed.

Every one of the castle's cannons had to be carried up the steep slopes by parties of 100 men to a gun. One party gave up and Christophe had half of the members executed on the spot.

After a reign of terror his fear-ridden subjects finally revolted in 1820 and stormed the mountain stronghold but Christophe, now half-paralysed, cheated them of their revenge by putting a bullet through his own twisted brain.

WHY THE CHICKEN CROSSED THE ROAD

Bob Walters, City Park Superintendent of Melbourne, Australia, was concerned about the high rate of casualties in a public park with traffic access. Despite the many stop signs and other conventional traffic control regulations, the rate of accidents showed no sign of dropping. Then Bob hit upon a bright idea, he obtained 86 chickens and put them at the park entrance just to strut about, but it had the desired effect of making the traffic move with much more caution with a dramatic fall in the accident rate.

Only occasionally does a madcap driver speed through the flock and in 1975, first year of the chicken patrol, only eight of the "traffic controllers" were killed.

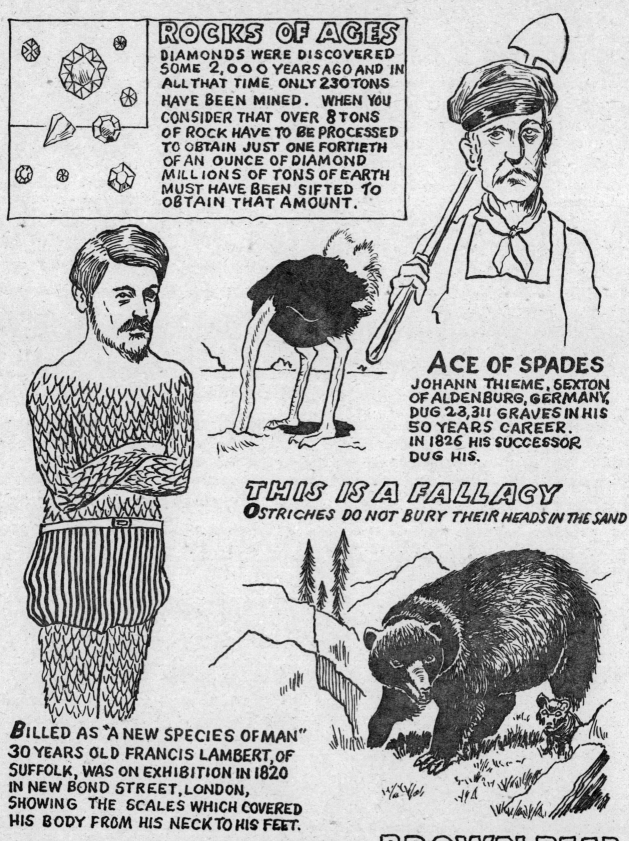

ROCKS OF AGES

DIAMONDS WERE DISCOVERED SOME 2,000 YEARS AGO AND IN ALL THAT TIME ONLY 230 TONS HAVE BEEN MINED. WHEN YOU CONSIDER THAT OVER 8 TONS OF ROCK HAVE TO BE PROCESSED TO OBTAIN JUST ONE FORTIETH OF AN OUNCE OF DIAMOND MILLIONS OF TONS OF EARTH MUST HAVE BEEN SIFTED TO OBTAIN THAT AMOUNT.

ACE OF SPADES

JOHANN THIEME, SEXTON OF ALDENBURG, GERMANY, DUG 23,311 GRAVES IN HIS 50 YEARS CAREER. IN 1826 HIS SUCCESSOR DUG HIS.

THIS IS A FALLACY

OSTRICHES DO NOT BURY THEIR HEADS IN THE SAND

BILLED AS "A NEW SPECIES OF MAN" 30 YEARS OLD FRANCIS LAMBERT, OF SUFFOLK, WAS ON EXHIBITION IN 1820 IN NEW BOND STREET, LONDON, SHOWING THE SCALES WHICH COVERED HIS BODY FROM HIS NECK TO HIS FEET.

A NEWBORN **BROWN BEAR** WEIGHS ONLY A POUND OR TWO BUT ITS MOTHER WEIGHS AROUND 20 STONES

KILLED-FOR AMUSEMENT

Competitors in modern athletic games can be assured that if they fail they won't become human torches or be thrown to the lions — but that was what used to happen to many of the people who took part in the ancient Roman games. These were held regularly over a 500 year period.

Men fought against wild animals, trained swordsmen against unarmed prisoners, women and children underwent terrible tortures and humiliations — all for the entertainment of the Roman citizenry.

The organisers of the "games" thought it great fun to put two men on a see-saw in the centre of the arena and then let in lions that had been starved for a few days.

Every time one of the victims touched down the hungry beasts would savage him until he could see-saw himself high into the air again.

The thousands of Christians who were sent to the arenas were singled out for very special treatment. Many were tied to the top of high stakes around the perimeter of the arena, pitch was poured over them and, as darkness fell, were lit to illuminate the ghastly scenes taking place in the ring.

Thousands of people were employed trapping and shipping wild animals of all kinds for "sport" in the arena. Among the huge assortment of beasts were giraffes, rhinos, elephants, the hippopotamus and even polar bears. When a foreign statesman visited Rome the best gift he could bring was wild animals.

One Roman Emperor, Marcus, spent a million pounds a year buying slaves to be trained as gladiators.

Some of the most exciting spectacles were the chariot races, which started originally as a sporting demonstration of skill but soon degenerated into cruel and brutal contests.

Most of the charioteers were slaves and could win a thousand pounds a race. The most successful ones, those who survived, won enough money to buy their freedom.

One such successful slave was Diocles, the first man to win 1,000 chariot races. He had an income a hundred times that of a senator, and enjoyed the idolatry given to pop stars of today. Crowds of girls would hang around his villa all day just to catch a glimpse of their idol. Publicans put up signs on their inns saying "Diocles ate here".

Sometimes hundreds of gladiators at a time fought hand-to-hand battles until the sand was soaked with blood. At one set of "games" which lasted 122 days and given by Emperor Trajan, 11,000 slaves and criminals and 10,000 animals of all kinds were slaughtered.

In the intervals between the various bouts the spectators would be showered with lottery tickets and there was great rivalry to grab one. A winning ticket could get the holder a prize such as a magnificent villa, a houseful of furniture or a beautiful slave girl.

But the warped sense of humour showed through with booby prizes. A person with a winning ticket would receive an ornate carved box. When opened up, a swarm of angry wasps would fly out in the face of the "winner"

Dog Boots

When the eighth Earl of Bridgewater, who died in 1829, came into a fortune of £40,000, he had a thing about boots. He ordered 365 pairs of boots and engaged a valet specially to look after them. He even had tiny boots made for his many dogs and insisted they wore them when they were being exercised.

* * *

Dry Land Sailor

Eccentric Yorkshireman, Jeremy Hirst, owned a boat but disliked sailing on the sea, so he had the craft mounted on wheels and sailed around most of the roads in his native country. He steered it with a tiller and when he was aboard wore a hat which was 9 ft around the brim.

* * *

* * *

The Pirate Archbishop

Launcelot Blackburne grew tired of his studies at Cambridge University so he upped and ran away to sea as a cabin boy. Pirates attacked and captured the ship he was on and he was pressed into their service. He enjoyed the adventurous life and rose to become a captain, and then deputy to the infamous Redmond of the Red Hand.

After making his fortune he returned to England and resumed his studies, gaining a degree at Cambridge and became a cleric.

In 1724, he was appointed Archbishop of York.

156

CONDEMNED HIMSELF TO DEATH!

Francis Lovell was one of England's richest men in the fifteenth century. In gratitude for his help and support in the Wars of the Roses, Richard III gave him the title of Viscount and gifts of money. He had a splendid manor built on the banks of the Windrush in Oxfordshire. Life for him was good and full.

But it didn't last long, two years later in 1485, Richard was slain at the Battle of Bosworth and the new king, Henry VII, stripped Lovell of power and political influence.

The Viscount then plotted and organised a rebellion which took place in 1487. It was a complete failure and Lovell became a wanted man.

Henry VII issued an order for his arrest and soldiers were sent to his grand home, Minster Lovell Hall, but he had vanished without trace. The whole of Southern England was scoured and people who had been close to him were tortured for information of his whereabouts but to no avail, no-one had seen him, no-one knew where he was.

His disappearance remained a mystery until two centuries later, in 1708, workmen who were making alterations to the house discovered an hitherto unknown vault under the floor. Generations of owners and servants had known nothing of its existence

It was Lovell's secret hideaway and, sat at the table piled with green mouldy paper was the skeleton of Lovell himself. He had deliberately shut himself in his chosen tomb and written his account of the abortive rebellion, then waited for death rather than face the disgrace and humiliation of trial and execution for treason.

LAST OF THE BIG CATS

45-50 YEARS AGO THERE WAS AN ESTIMATED 50,000 TIGERS IN INDIA ~ TODAY THERE'S ABOUT 2,000 LEFT.

GALLEY SLAVE
FOR A CENTURY!

JEAN BAPTISTE MOURON OF TOULON, FRANCE, CONVICTED OF ARSON IN 1684, WAS SENTENCED TO 100 YEARS AND A DAY IN THE GALLEYS - AND SERVED EVERY DAY OF IT!

HE WAS 17 WHEN HE STARTED HIS SENTENCE AND DIED SIX YEARS AFTER HIS RELEASE.

THE MOST COSTLY DRESS

WAS MADE FOR MARIE DE MEDICI (1573-1643) QUEEN OF FRANCE. IT WAS EMBROIDERED WITH 3,000 DIAMONDS AND 39,000 PEARLS.

AT TODAY'S VALUES A CONSERVATIVE ESTIMATE IT WOULD BE WORTH IN THE REGION OF £9 TO 10,000,000.

YET SHE WORE IT ONLY ONCE - AT THE BAPTISM OF HER SON, SEPT. 14th. 1606

EXPENSIVE BET

Finn Nils Roskov wagered with a friend that he could run 100 metres while balancing 20 boxes on his head. The bet was for £8.

All went well until he neared the end of the run when an apparently short-sighted pigeon flew into the boxes scattering them all over the place. Unfortunately the top boxes landed on the heads of two horses pulling a brewer's dray. The horses promptly panicked and bolted off down the street, bouncing the dray off several parked cars, causing £340 work of damage.

Nils, a market porter of Helsinki, Finland, lost the bet and had to pay for the damaged cars.

The Tracks of Time

With the exception of the USSR, almost the entire civilised world uses the standard railway gauge of 4 ft 8½ ins as laid down by the first British railways.

How did the first railways settle on this particular width? The answer lies in the width of the Roman chariots used by Julius Caesar's army in the invasion of Britain in 55 BC. The native Britons copied the invaders chariots when building more peaceful vehicles, the ruts left by the wheels were just 4 ft 8½ ins wide. This was adopted by the railway builders centuries after Caesar's invasion — the indelible tracks of history.

The USSR National Railway had a total workforce of 2,031,200 employees in 1976 — the greatest payroll of any civilian organisation in the world.

Union Power

We are well acquainted with unions in Britain but nothing like the unions that used to exist in China. There was the Thieves Union or Guild which knew the state of the market for stolen goods, and the best area for thieves to work in. Those with special talents, safe-cracking, etc, were directed to places where these talents could be of most use. In Shanghai the Guild ran thieving like a business and merchants and private people paid "insurance" to ensure that their premises did not attract the attention of Guild members. There was always a waiting list of applicants who were expected to pay "dues" and give guarantees of good conduct and proficiency until they were "taken on to the books".

Beggars had their own union too. The Guild would send out "talent scouts" up-country to enlist likely members. To qualify the would-be union members had to have sores, leprosy or other spectacular physical defects. Sometimes parents would deliberately disfigure or maim their own children so that they could become beggars.

Recruits would be given special training in the art of begging and allotted districts to which they were most suited, and of course, they paid their dues to the union.

Like their brothers in the Thieves Guild, the Beggars were paid handsomely by shopkeepers to be free of their members' attentions. Woe betide any shop that refused a donation. Hordes of filthy, deformed, blind beggars would invade the premises, banging gongs and generally disrupting business until their demands were met, it didn't usually happen more than once.

They even went on a 48 hours strike in sympathy with students protesting about the influx of Japanese goods. Several beggars' organisations contributed generously to Famine Relief Fund.

A missionary doctor, working amongst the poor, operated on a poor blind beggar and cured him of a cataract. He was told in no uncertain terms that he had taken away the only means of making a living the man had, and it was his duty to give him the job as gatekeeper of the hospital.

Of course, under the new system, organisations like that could no longer exist.

The WORLD'S MEANEST WOMAN

The old woman rarely washed, didn't change her clothes for months on end and ate a meal of cold porridge a day. When her son was crippled in a fall, she stuffed his clothes with newspapers to keep him warm and toted him around some thirty free treatment clinics to save doctors' bills, but it didn't save the boy's leg, he eventually had to have it amputated.

Yet this woman, Hetty Green, who lived in the America of the late 19th century, amassed a tremendous fortune of $100 million, a massive amount in these days but then worth many times more.

She demanded, and got, the use of a desk in a bank from where she operated her money making activities, shocking even the hard-boiled stockbrokers of America with her wheeling and dealing. She even forged documents to get more and more money and ran a mortgage business inflicting misery on the many owners of small businesses and homes.

When the wretched woman died, her crippled son, Ned, spent, spent and spent. He bought his mistress a £50,000 chastity belt and installed 12 pretty young secretaries and a masseuse in a suite at the Waldorf-Astoria Hotel at a rent of £600 a week. He spent £150,000 refurnishing the room and further £2,000,000 on jewellery, he even had a ruby-studded chamber-pot.

He had private railway coaches built and his steam yacht fitted at a cost of £2,000,000. He always carried wads of $10,000 bills to the value of a quarter of a million pounds. His weird sense of humour showed itself when he despatched two battered cardboard boxes tied up with string, by rail. He 'phoned the rail company and told them the boxes contained two million dollars in cash and jewels. After a frantic search the boxes were found on the back of an open lorry parked outside a cafe. The driver was inside, unaware of the treasure he was carrying.

When Ned Green died in 1936 aged 67, it took 200 lawyers, 385 witnesses and 4,000,000 words of evidence to sort out the estate over twenty-nine months. His sister Sylvia spent the last three years of her life dividing her share up with one of the most complicated wills of all time.

The BLACK SWALLOWER,

WHICH LIVES OFF THE COAST OF BERMUDA, IS CAPABLE OF SWALLOWING A FISH THREE TIMES ITS OWN SIZE, ITS STOMACH DISTENDING TO AN ENORMOUS SIZE.

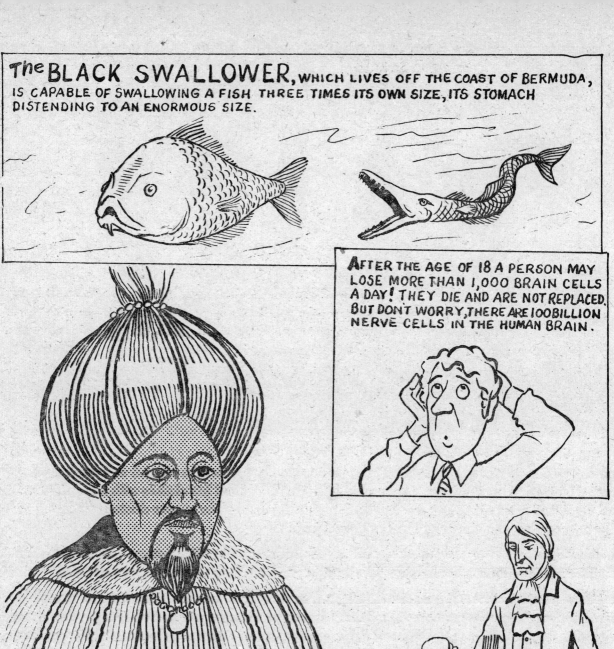

AFTER THE AGE OF 18 A PERSON MAY LOSE MORE THAN 1,000 BRAIN CELLS A DAY! THEY DIE AND ARE NOT REPLACED. BUT DON'T WORRY, THERE ARE 100 BILLION NERVE CELLS IN THE HUMAN BRAIN.

SULTAN MUSTAPHA III

OF TURKEY (1717-1774) FATHERED 582 CHILDREN — EVERY ONE A BOY! HE PROMISED THE EXALTED TITLE OF EMPRESS TO ANY OF HIS CONCUBINES WHO COULD PRESENT HIM WITH A DAUGHTER — NONE EVER DID.

VAULT IN THE BANK

AN 8 FT. TALL GIANT, JENKINS, A CLERK AT THE BANK OF ENGLAND, WHO DIED IN 1798, REQUESTED THAT, TO FOIL BODY SNATCHERS, HE BE BURIED IN THE SAFEST PLACE HE KNEW ~ THE BANK PREMISES. HIS REQUEST WAS GRANTED.

Gentlemen, You May Smoke

In Prussia, in 1848, it was forbidden to smoke in the street. A fine was imposed for a first offence, a second led to jail and a third offence could land the culprit in jail for 5 years!

But the restriction almost toppled a throne. Prussian workmen staged a revolt in defence of their right to smoke in public. A huge crowd gathered outside the royal palace chanting "Liberty to smoke in public". The military wanted to call out the troops, but the young Prince Lichnovsky feared that a bloody massacre might result, so he ordered a table to be placed on the balcony. Standing on the table, the Prince raised his arms for silence. The mob below fell silent. Taking a cigar from his pocket, he lit up then said "Your liberty has been granted". The crowd cheered and a cloud of smoke arose as they peacefully dispersed.

Strangely enough, exactly the opposite was happening at the same time in Milan. The people of Milan, who were ruled by the Austrians, refused to smoke at all, to annoy their rulers and to deprive them of the huge revenue that the tax on tobacco brought in. Overnight, posters and placards appeared all over the city with the warning "Only Germans and spies smoke tobacco". And the citizens didn't content themselves with just written protests. Anyone seen smoking had their cigars or pipes knocked out of their mouths — even the occupation forces.

When news of the ban reached the Austrian commander-in-chief, he ordered a free issue of tobacco and cigars to his troops, he then sent them round the town puffing away for all they were worth.

Things began to take a turn for the worse when the revolt spread to Pavia. There, a student was shot on the spot when he knocked the cigar from a soldier's mouth.

The revolt spread throughout Italy. It reached Venice where there was a huge store of Virginian cigars, and then to Piedmont where the population took up arms and opposed the Austrian troops.

They were obliged to evacuate all soldiers from Milan, and the revolt only ended when crowds of citizens seized and burnt millions of cigars in the warehouses.

Over a century ago riots took place in Edinburgh, which were touched-off by Puritans who wanted smoking forbidden in the streets on the Sabbath. As a protest, a crowd of students marched up and down outside the Puritans' homes and through the city carrying torches which gave off an evil-smelling odour.

After a couple of days the anti-smoking leaders relented and dropped the idea. Unfortunately, the protest march caused a fire in which 17 people lost their lives.

In some colonies in America, where tobacco smoking originated, Puritans banned all smoking, drinking and kissing in public. A few hardy individuals retaliated by lighting bonfires around the Puritans' municipal headquarters. Guards who were sent out were subjected to attacks.

Finally, smoking was allowed but the ban on drinking and kissing in public remained.

SHOUT STARTED MASSACRE

Christmas Day, 1066, saw the first coronation of a king at Westminster Abbey. It was, of course, that of William the Conqueror, but the day ended in tragedy through a misunderstanding.

After the Archbishop of York had placed the crown on William's head, he asked the assembled Saxon nobles if they would recognise the King as their true liege lord. The shout of acclamation that went up so alarmed the Norman soldiers on guard outside, that they took it as a cry of rejection and dashed into the congregation with drawn swords and attacked them.

Very soon the fighting spread to the crowd outside and by the end of the day the streets of London were strewn with the bodies of the dead and dying illuminated by the glare of burning houses.

William's grandson, Stephen, postponed his coronation from Christmas Day to Boxing Day to avoid a possible recurrence of the tragedy.

On the eve of his coronation Stephen provided a sumptuous feast for his nobles and citizens of London, believing probably, that a full stomach would cure any feelings of animosity.

As it turned out, it was the happiest day of his reign, it being described as the most miserable in English history.

While he was fighting his cousin, Matilda, for the crown, the Norman barons were busy forcing the Saxons to build castles for them and extorting money from all and sundry under threat of torture. It is said a man could travel a day's walk without seeing a tilled field or an inhabited township. The Normans looted town and country.

Yet Stephen was a brave, kindly man, but too good-natured and easily fooled.

When King John ascended the throne in 1199, he gave one of the most fantastic Christmas parties ever recorded. 200 gallons of various wines, 400 oxen, 1,000 capons, 1,000 eels and 200 lampreys were devoured by his hungry guests.

Not surprisingly, John died of over-eating in 1216, a fugitive from his enemies.

PHANTOM CITY

Bristol is some 4,500 miles from Alaska and yet, by some strange trick of nature, images of the English city are seen in the same three-week period every year in the sky over Alaska.

Between June 21st and July 10th the phantom city is said to have been seen each year by the native Alaskan Indians long before the white man arrived.

Since then people who have seen the phenomenom and who know Bristol have identified it as that city.

Another similar mirage was seen by the crew of an ice-breaker on New Years Eve 1946, in the Atlantic. They saw an American city pictured on a cloud. The original was thousands of miles away.

GRAVE WORDS

AMERICAN PASTOR JAMES DOTSON, WHO DIED 1st FEB. 1983, AGED 27, DELIVERED THE SERMON AT HIS OWN FUNERAL AT MANSFIELD, OHIO — ON VIDEOTAPE.

FIRST CROSS CHANNEL FLIGHT

WAS MADE BY BLANCHARD AND JEFFRIES ON JAN. 7th 1785. THE TRIP TOOK TWO HOURS AND THE TWO BALLOONISTS WERE OBLIGED TO JETTISON MOST OF THEIR CLOTHES TO PREVENT THEIR CRAFT FROM LOSING HEIGHT.

PRINCE ORLOF,

A RUSSIAN ARISTOCRAT AT THE COURT OF CATHERINE THE GREAT, WORE A COAT OF PURE SPUN GOLD WORTH, AT TODAY'S VALUES, OVER TWENTY MILLION POUNDS.

TIMID TIGER

THE BARBARY MOUSE, OF NORTH AFRICA, HAS STRIPES SIMILAR TO THOSE OF A TIGER.

SOLE SURVIVOR - ONE HORSE.

As the U.S. cavalry relief force surveyed the scene of carnage in the Valley of the Little Bighorn not a living thing moved until a single horse, blood spattered and weak, struggled to get to its feet. It was the sole survivor of Custer's last stand when 264 soldiers of the 7th U.S. Cavalry were surrounded and annihilated by the braves of Chief Sitting Bull on June 25th. 1876.

The horse, named "Commanche," was lovingly nursed back to health and became the mascot of the regiment with the title of second-in-command. But when Korn, his handler, was killed in 1890 in one of the final Indian campaigns, Commanche died of a broken heart a few months later at the age of 29. His stuffed body can still be seen in the University of Kansas.

You may not have a 'skeleton in the closet' but you probably have one in the bathroom. The loofah is the skeleton of a cucumber-like sea plant.

ST. ENCUMBER,

THE PATRON SAINT OF BEARDS, IS SAID TO HAVE MIRACULOUSLY SPROUTED A BEARD WHEN THE YOUNG VIRGIN'S FATHER TRIED TO MARRY HER OFF TO AN UNWANTED SUITOR.

Riding High

When you see Indians riding horses in westerns it's assumed that the horse is native to America, not so! The prehistoric horse of the North American continent was about the size of a dog and became extinct many centuries before the white man arrived.

The horses, which the Indians rode, are descended from the horses brought over by the Spanish explorers and missionaries in the 16th century. They traded or gave the horses to the Indians who soon learned to breed and ride them. So, by the time the settlers from the east came, they were experts in horsemanship.

Today there are about 72 million horses in the USA!

PAUL HUBERT
OF BORDEAUX, FRANCE, SPENT 21 YEARS IN SOLITARY CONFINEMENT BEFORE IT WAS DISCOVERED THAT HIS SUPPOSED VICTIM WAS NONE OTHER THAN HIMSELF!

KING GRASS
THE BAMBOO WHICH GROWS ON THE MALAY PENINSULA AND REACHES A HEIGHT OF 120 FEET, IS REALLY A SPECIES OF GRASS AND IN FACT IS KNOWN AS "THE KING OF GRASSES."

MORE THAN **90%** OF ALL SPECIES OF FLOWERS IN THE WORLD HAVE NO SMELL AT ALL OR AN UNPLEASANT ODOUR!

Trip to the Past

On holiday together in Paris, the two English school mistresses decided to visit the Palace of Versailles one August day in 1901 and, accordingly, toured the State Apartments, guide book in hand.

Eventually, they left the Palace, intending to visit the Petit Trianon – a little château in the grounds that was once the retreat of the ill-fated Marie Antoinette. Miss Annie Moberly and Miss Eleanor Jourdain were about to embark on an extraordinary journey into the past.

Instead of taking the usual tourist route – the Allée des Deux Trianons – they took a shady, sunken path to the right of the Grand Trianon forecourt which led directly to the gardener's gate into the grounds of the Petit Trianon. It was shortly after 4 pm when the two friends stepped through the gate into a mystery.

On their journey through the grounds they "met" eight people, including Marie Antoinette, who had been dead for a century, and passed landmarks which had long-since gone. They noticed the absence of any other sightseers but they walked on in silence with a strange feeling of isolation. Eventually they came to a crossroads of three paths – they went along the middle – because they saw two men further along, standing near a wheelbarrow and who they took to be gardeners.

As they approached the two men, who were deep in conversation, they noticed that the men were dressed in long grey-green coats and old-fashioned three cornered hats. Miss Jourdain asked them the way to the house and was told brusquely "Go straight on".

And on they went, past a cottage, with a woman and girl standing outside, dressed in old fashioned dresses and seeming strangely motionless. Next, they came to a clump of trees with a garden kiosk beneath them and, sitting on the steps, the most evil-looking man they had ever seen, his swarthy face heavily pock-marked. He wore a black coat and a large black hat.

Suddenly, they heard the sound of running footsteps. Appearing as if from nowhere, they saw a man coming towards them, he too, was dressed in similar clothes to the man in the kiosk. "Mesdames" he gasped, "It is not permitted for you to pass here. Go to the house."

They followed the direction he had indicated, over a small bridge, past a foaming cascade, and came to the Petit Trianon. Sitting below the terrace, sketching busily, was a woman who Miss Moberly "identified" as Marie Antoinette.

They continued up the steps on to the terrace. A door opened suddenly and a young footman appeared, the footman ushered them through to the front of the house – then disappeared.

As they stepped through the front door they stepped back into reality. They found a group of sightseers and their depression lifted

Miss Moberly and Miss Jourdain talked it over later and found that each had seen some people the other hadn't – though they hadn't been separated.

The day of their visit had been the 10th of August, the anniversary of the day on which an angry mob had invaded the Palace and grounds.

After much research they discovered that a messenger had been hurriedly sent to warn the Queen – the man they had seen running in the garden?

The evil-looking man in the garden kiosk could have been no other than the Comte de Vaudreuil, a creole who had been a confidante of the Queen, but had eventually betrayed her. The two men who they thought were gardeners could have been the special Swiss guard who kept watch when the Queen was in residence at the Petit Trianon.

Other people had reported seeing the Queen in the grounds and also the courtiers.

Had the two ladies really been transported to the past or, as sceptics say, had they a very lively imagination? It's something that can't be proved, but it makes one wonder.

The Halifax Gibbet

For at least two centuries, before the French Revolution, the guillotine was in use in Yorkshire. The device was known as the Halifax Gibbet and was similar to the later French model. During the 16th and part of the 17th century, any person taken for stealing within the boundaries of the forest of Hardwick, near Halifax, was put in the stocks for 3 market days with the stolen goods displayed either on his back or in front of him. After this period the convicted person was sentenced "to be carried to the gibbet and there have his head cut from his body".

Should the thief have stolen an animal, such as a horse or a cow, the animal was taken with him and tied to the pin holding the blade in place. The animal would be driven forward, pulling the pin out and so releasing the blade to drop on the thief's neck.

Although records have been lost for the period before the reign of Elizabeth I some 35 people met their deaths by this method up to the year 1650.

A Square Drink

Astronauts have proved that man can survive pretty well on concentrated foods in the form of pills. In time perhaps all of us will be able to have a slap-up meal by popping a couple of pills.

But nothing is really new under the sun. In 1761 an Oxford pedlar used to sell concentrated beer in cubes, not unlike a beef cube. The buyer simply dropped a cube in a tankard of water to produce a very strong porter.

The cubes were advertised as "a tankard of beer on a teaspoon" and were very popular with the young men of the time who would carry the cubes in their waistcoat pockets.

★ ★ ★ ★

The bells of Toul Cathedral, France, were rung for 40 days and nights to mourn the death of Louis XV. The bell tower was so weakened by the vibration that its swaying kept the bells ringing for the next 20 years 7 months.

HOMECOMING

CHARLES COUGHLIN, A TOURING ACTOR, DIED
IN 1899 AND WAS BURIED IN GALVESTON, TEXAS, U.S.A.
ON SEPT. 8TH 1900, A TERRIFIC HURRICANE HIT
THE AREA, DEVASTATING, AMONG OTHER THINGS,
THE GRAVEYARD. COUGHLIN'S COFFIN WAS
WASHED OUT OF ITS GRAVE AND CARRIED
OUT TO SEA WITH ITS OCCUPANT.
AFTER TRAVELLING 2,000 MILES IT
EVENTUALLY CAME TO REST
ON PRINCE EDWARD ISLAND,
CANADA—*THE PLACE
WHERE HE WAS BORN!*

BLOODBATH

HUNGARIAN NOBLEWOMAN, COUNTESS ELIZABETH
B'ATHORY (1560-1614) WAS RESPONSIBLE FOR THE DEATHS
OF 650 SERVANT GIRLS OVER A PERIOD OF 6 YEARS. SHE
USED TO BATHE IN THE BLOOD OF HER UNFORTUNATE VICTIMS
IN THE BELIEF THAT IT PRESERVED HER YOUTH AND BEAUTY.

THE DISAPPEARANCE OF SO MANY YOUNG
MAIDENS ALARMED THE AUTHORITIES
AND EVENTUALLY THE TRAIL LED TO THE
COUNTESS, BUT THE SNAG WAS, BEING OF
NOBLE BLOOD, THE FULL FORCE OF THE LAW
COULD NOT BE APPLIED. INSTEAD SHE WAS
WALLED UP IN HER BEDROOM FOR THE REMAINDER
OF HER LIFE.

WARRIOR FEATHERS

THE SPECIALLY BRED
ONAGADORI COCK,
OF JAPAN, ATTAIN
TAIL FEATHERS 30 FT.
LONG.

SAMURAI WARRIORS
USED TO ADORN
THEMSELVES IN
ONAGADORI FEATHERS.

Just a Word

One of the longest titles ever given to a book was an American publication about how to write best-sellers in one's spare time. The title consisted of forty-three words.

Just about the shortest book title was a novel published in Britain and entitled "B". It consisted of three volumes.

Now, what about the shortest books? Before World War II a French newspaper offered a prize of 10,000 francs for the most original book. The prize was won by a Yugoslav with a book called "Who Rules the World?" The manuscript he submitted contained just one word "Money". The newspaper claimed his entry as unique, paid the prize-money and published the book. It ran to many editions and became a best-seller!

Another odd book was by a retired admiral some years ago. He had spent some time in China and was given a farewell dinner by some residents before returning to Europe. As a farewell gift to his hosts he gave each a book bearing his name as author. It was entitled "What I know about China" — every page in the book was blank!

It is estimated that the world population in 1982 was 4,580,000,000. The population increases by 232,800 a day or 161 every minute!

In the last 600,000 years, around 75,000,000,000 people have been born and died.

In the Province of Macau on the south coast of China, there are 44,350 people per square mile. The most densely populated part of Britain is the Greater London Borough of Kensington and Chelsea with 5,312 people per km² or 13,292 per square mile.

The least populated parts of the UK are the Scottish Highlands and Islands with about 5 people per square mile.

Odd Cures

Here's a list of some ancient cures which frankly should make your flesh creep even if it doesn't effect a cure. The ancients were odd people. Here are the cures as written down.

Aspen leaves are considered good against ague.

Snails boiled in barley water are a sovereign cure for an ordinary cough.

Whooping cough can be cured by anyone riding on a piebald horse.

The heart-shaped leaves of the ordinary wood sorrel were remedial in cardiac disease.

Tumeric, on account of its deep yellow colour, was of great reputation in the treatment of jaundice.

Anyone suffering the agonies of toothache was instantly relieved by merely smelling a dead man's tooth.

Driving an iron nail into an oak tree, a sure cure for toothache.

A little moss growing on a skull, dried well, and used as snuff, was specific for headache.

Warts, put 3 drops of the blood of a wart into an eldern leaf and bury it in the earth and the warts will vanish away.

The powdered flesh of a mummy was of sovereign power in physic, especially in contusions, where it prevented the blood from settling and coagulating at the injured part.

The flowers of the Lily of the Valley being closely stopped up in glass, put into an anthill and taken away a month later, ye shall find a liquor in the glass, which, being outwardly applied, helpeth gout.

Chilblains should be rubbed well with a mouse skin, or the sufferer should roll his feet and ankles in hot embers.

Aren't you glad you weren't about in olden times?

GHOST PLANE

It was wartime, 1941, the Battle of Britain had been fought and won when the Spitfire pilot, returning from a routine patrol over a lonely part of the Scottish coast, spotted a strange bi-plane ahead of him. As he picked up speed to investigate, the pilot was amazed to find the stranger was keeping way ahead of him. Opening full out to around 350 mph the fastest speed of any warplane at that time, he was more than amazed when, at top speed, his Spitfire just could not catch it up.

Discussing the event later with his fellow officers, each one a hardened veteran of the recent air battles, he found that the mystery aircraft had been seen and reported several times.

The unusual thing was that the unidentified aircraft appeared whenever there was some threat to the area: a raid by a German bomber on the airfield, a U-boat two miles off shore, Junkers 88 fighter-bomber awaiting for the return of planes from patrol and so on. Each time the bi-plane made an appearance, attracting the notice of the pilots to the danger.

The mystery remained until a patrolling Spitfire spotted the shape of a grounded aircraft in a secluded valley. He immediately reported its position back to base and a land rescue was sent out.

It took them several days of rugged travel before they came to the plane. It was a Sopwith Camel vintage 1917 — the mystery guardian of the lonely RAF base. The ancient plane was in a remarkably undamaged condition except for the usual wear of time and weather, but in the cockpit, as if still at the controls, sat the grinning skeleton of the pilot, tatters of his First World War uniform hanging from the whitened bones.

The number of the aircraft was clearly discernable and subsequent investigation revealed the long dead aviator and identified him as an RNAS pilot who had taken off one day in 1917 on patrol and never returned.

Mechanics who examined the machine found that a petrol blockage had caused an engine failure, forcing the pilot to make an emergency landing; unfortunately the wheels had snagged in a small gully throwing the luckless airman forward and according to the doctors' report, breaking both his legs, consequently trapping him in the cockpit. Unable to leave his seat to repair the engine, a simple five or ten minute job, and having no radio to summon help, he had slowly starved to death, hope dwindling as each day passed. His rescuers arrived 22 years too late.

Once the remains of the man had been removed and buried, the lone patrol of the ghost plane ceased and it was never seen again, another of the world's inexplicable mysteries.

SOME NECK

300 SCHOOLCHILDREN IN SWEDEN FELT SO SORRY FOR KONRAD, A GIRAFFE IN A ZOO NEAR STOCKHOLM, THAT THEY KNITTED A SCARF 75 FEET LONG TO KEEP HIS NECK WARM IN THE WINTER.

ROYAL FORGER

HENRY VIII, ALWAYS ON THE LOOKOUT FOR SWELLING THE ROYAL COFFERS, ISSUED "SILVER" TESTOONS WHICH IF FACT WERE COPPER COINS WITH A THIN COATING OF SILVER. AS THE SILVER COVERING WORE OFF THE KING'S COPPER NOSE SHOWED THROUGH EARNING HIM THE NICK-NAME OF "OLD KING COPPERNOB" TODAY ONE SPECIMEN OF THESE DEBASED OOINS WOULD FETCH WELL OVER £100.

COUNTDOWN

NO RELIABLE CENSUS OF THE POPULATION OF CHINA HAS BEEN TAKEN SINCE 1402-03 WHEN THE RULING EMPEROR-USING THE DEATH PENALTY AS A THREAT-TOOK A COUNT IN 1402 WHEN THE FIGURE WAS GIVEN AS 56,301,026. BY 1403 THIS FIGURE HAD INCREASED TO 66,598,337.
TODAY THE POPULATION OF CHINA HAS BEEN ESTIMATED AT OVER 850,000,000.
AND WILL NUMBER HALF THE WORLD'S POPULATION BY THE END OF THE CENTURY.

The BIGGEST FEAST IN HISTORY

To celebrate his victory over Pompey, Julius Caesar gave a banquet at which 150,000 guests were seated at 22,000 tables. It lasted for 2 days. He also proclaimed a rent-free year for every poor family in the Empire.

TIP TOE THROUGH THE TURBANS!
YOU PROBABLY THINK THAT THE TULIP ORIGINATED IN HOLLAND BUT THE FLOWER ACTUALLY CAME FROM THE TURKISH AREA AND DIDN'T REACH HOLLAND UNTIL 1562. THE WORD TULIP COMES FROM A TURKISH WORD MEANING "TURBAN"

TRUFFLES, A BLACK FUNGI WHICH GROWS UNDERGROUND IN FRANCE AND ITALY, ARE THE MOST COSTLY SINGLE FOOD ITEM AT WELL OVER £100 A POUND AND IS USED TO FLAVOUR SAUCES. FARMERS TRAIN PIGS TO ROOT OUT THE TRUFFLES.

GRANNY AT 17!
MUM-ZI, FAVOURITE WIFE OF CHIEF AKKIRI ON THE ISLAND OF CALABAR, AFRICA, BECAME A GRANDMOTHER AT THE AGE OF SEVENTEEN. SHE BORE A DAUGHTER AT THE AGE OF 8 YEARS AND 4 MONTHS. IN TURN HER DAUGHTER BORE A CHILD AT THE SAME AGE.

The SILVER SEA
SIR FRANCIS DRAKE WAS OBLIGED TO DUMP TONS OF SILVER BARS INTO THE SEA OFF PLATE ISLAND IN ORDER TO LIGHTEN HIS SHIP "THE GOLDEN HIND."

BATTLE OF THE GHOSTS

Farmworkers on their way home from work from Banbury to Kineton in Warwickshire, were astounded to see and hear what amounted to an action replay of the Battle of Edgehill which had been fought three months earlier in October 1642, between the Roundheads and Cavaliers in the Civil War.

For two hours, the terrified country people watched the amazing battle in the sky. The flash and crash of cannon, the ring of sword upon steel, the screams of wounded men and horses were clearly heard. They saw the cavalry and infantry engaged in desperate conflict, flags flying and swords glinting. More soldiers advanced from the sky in the north, and then the phantom battle scene faded.

The terrifying occurrence was reported and the next night an investigatory party, led by a magistrate and a clergyman, witnessed yet another replay of the battle.

King Charles I, then with his army at Oxford, sent six of his officers to investigate. These officers witnessed the battle on two successive nights, they even recognised some of their dead comrades amongst the ghostly hosts. They testified that the battle in the sky happened as it did in reality.

Their report is probably the only ghost story accepted in the documents of the Public Records Office as authentic.

Warrior Queen

Presutagus, King of the Iceni, whose territory covered what is now Norfolk and Suffolk, fought with Roman invaders fiercely, protecting his kingdom, and, as a tribute to his gallantry in battle, the Romans allowed him to remain king in his domain. As a protection for his family and Queen, Boadicea, he willed his territory to Emperor Nero on his death, but with a proviso that Boadicea would continue as Queen.

The Romans kept their word, but as soon as the old warrior died, they imposed severe taxes on the people, even on the British corpses. They were forced to borrow money from Roman moneylenders until they became little more than slaves.

The tribe's eventual inability to pay their dues led to orders being given to punish the Queen. Soldiers forced their way into the royal house, killing her bodyguard and violating her daughters. The Queen herself was tied to a post and flogged and the house pillaged.

The anger of the Iceni spread far and wide inflaming even the Trinobantes who lived in neighbouring areas, now Essex and Middlesex. Suetonius Paulinus, the Roman governor, was unaware of the revolt that was brewing, he was too busy exterminating the troublesome Brigantes in the north and the Druid priests on Anglesey 200 miles away.

In the south-east of England, the Roman garrisons were at Colchester, London and St Albans while the much vaunted 9th Legion was encamped near the Wash. It was then that the Queen, her heart full of revenge, struck, at the head of her tribe. The Britons fought savagely, no Roman they came across was spared. The revolt spread and Boadicea turned her attention to London, now crowded with Roman refugees from surrounding country towns and villas.

Governor Suetonius was but a few miles away when the rampaging Britons descended on London but astute Suetonius wouldn't risk his weary legions against the triumphant Britons so he left London at the mercy of the hate-filled warriors, and marched off to Essex to prepare for a last stand.

About 100,000 had been killed by now and the slaughter continued as the victorious British followed the vengeful Queen to Essex to battle with the 10,000 legionaires waiting there. If they won it would mean the end of Roman rule in Britain.

But the Romans were ready for them. They had chosen carefully where they would meet their foes. It was a narrow valley, and company after company waited like a great armoured wedge, the Britons could only attack with just a few battalions at a time. The Romans slaughtered them. About 80,000 men, women and children died by the Roman sword and pilum; they were merciless.

Boadicea drove from the scene of carnage in her chariot, her heart heavy at the deaths of her countrymen. It's not certain as to whether she was handed over by a Queen of the Brigantes, but she did fall into the Romans' hands and died from taking poison, probably self-administered. The brave Queen had come so close to defeating the might of Rome.

Curiously, she is believed to be buried on a site now covered by number 10 platform of King's Cross Station.

Stop! Thief . . .

The village of Mina in the middle of India's Rajasthan desert is the strangest on earth — or rather the villagers are. Every one is a thief! Stealing is their traditional occupation.

But, according to their own peculiar standards, they are honourable crooks. A Mina will take a domestic job with a rich family, but he never steals from his employers, oh no, instead he passes on any information he extracts from the servants of neighbouring wealthy families. This is passed back to the village and very soon a fellow Mina arrives to carry out a job on the neighbour's house.

They always make a point of travelling first class on their criminal expeditions. Money or jewellery is their favourite target, and then the job is done, they quickly leave the scene of the crime either by train or plane and sell the proceeds of the robbery.

The police, of course, don't share the Mina's adherence to their tradition and their pressure is making burglary a very tricky occupation. Many of the Minas wish to take up an honest job but they say as soon as people learn where they come from they meet with immediate distrust. Not really surprising, is it?

We in England are used to the more gentle rainfall but it can rain here with something like the force of the rains of tropical parts. In a day and a night in 1912 sixty million tons of rain fell on one part of Norfolk, one of the greatest rainstorms ever seen in this country.

In July 1901, 3.63 inches of rain fell at Maidenhead, Berkshire, in only one hour. At Bruton in Somerset, the equivalent of 965 tons of rain per acre fell in one day in June 1917, and for 89 days rain fell every day at Eallabus, Isle of Islay, Western Scotland, the longest-ever spell of rain in Britain.

In California, some years ago, rain fell at the rate of 1.03 inches a minute. That would fill a bath faster than having two taps running full on.

Hailstones can also create havoc. The world over farmers dread the destruction and devastation which these icy bombardments can bring. In the June of 1983, Georgia, USSR was struck by a terrific hailstorm and thousands of cattle were killed in the fields by the huge chunks of ice which fell from the sky, vast areas of fruit trees were stripped bare. In a bad year British growers can lose more than a million pounds worth of crops due to hail damage.

Hailstones are classified by size: pea, mothball, marble, ping-pong ball, goose egg, tennis ball and melon. Hailstones are formed every time raindrops are sucked into the upper layers of cloud where they get a coating of ice, eventually these millions of bits of ice are released in a cloudburst. A big raincloud can weigh as much as the QE2.

In Delhi, India, in the 1880's nearly 250 people died in a fall of chunks of ice or were buried under drifts that froze solid.

A group of five Germans gliding thousands of feet above the earth were sucked into a huge cloud by a fierce updraught. Fearing that their glider would be smashed to bits by hailstones, they baled out. When they came down to earth, four of them were found to be dead, encased in coffins of ice.

THE MAN WITH THE GOLDEN NOSE

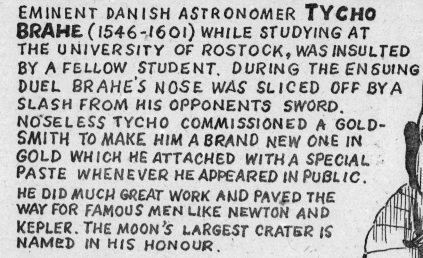

EMINENT DANISH ASTRONOMER **TYCHO BRAHE** (1546-1601) WHILE STUDYING AT THE UNIVERSITY OF ROSTOCK, WAS INSULTED BY A FELLOW STUDENT. DURING THE ENSUING DUEL BRAHE'S NOSE WAS SLICED OFF BY A SLASH FROM HIS OPPONENTS SWORD. NOSELESS TYCHO COMMISSIONED A GOLD-SMITH TO MAKE HIM A BRAND NEW ONE IN GOLD WHICH HE ATTACHED WITH A SPECIAL PASTE WHENEVER HE APPEARED IN PUBLIC.

HE DID MUCH GREAT WORK AND PAVED THE WAY FOR FAMOUS MEN LIKE NEWTON AND KEPLER. THE MOON'S LARGEST CRATER IS NAMED IN HIS HONOUR.

HAIL AND FAREWELL!

GIANT HAILSTONES, SOME WEIGHING AS MUCH AS 6 lbs. FELL DURING A STORM IN THE PROVINCE OF HUNAN, CHINA, IN MAY 1983, KILLING 81 PEOPLE, SHATTERING ROOFS, FLATTENING THE RICE CROP AND SLICING FRUIT FROM THE TREES.

THE APTLY NAMED
TAILOR BIRD

OF INDIA AND CHINA, AFTER SELECTING A SUITABLE LEAF, ACTUALLY SEWS THE EDGES NEATLY TOGETHER WITH FIBRE THUS FORMING A POCKET IN WHICH IT BUILDS ITS NEST.

Worth Their Weight in Gold

Persian poet, Abul Feizi Hindi, personal tutor to the three sons of Akbar, Emperor of India, was paid annually for 15 years, the equivalent sum in gold of the combined weight of his three students. No doubt he didn't ban them from eating sweets in class!

✶ ✶ ✶ ✶ ✶

Tiny Duelist

Jeffrey Hudson, born in Oakham, Rutland, entered the service of the Duke of Buckingham at the age of nine, when he was only 18 ins tall.

Shortly after Charles the First's marriage to Henrietta Maria, Jeffrey was presented to the Queen in a novel way — he was served up in a cold pie!

He became known as the Queen's dwarf and fought in the Civil War as a commissioned officer, killed a man in a duel and even fought a duel with a turkey-cock.

He was captured by Turkish pirates and the rigours of his harsh captivity caused him to grow to 3 ft 9 ins when he was thirty.

He was later thrown into jail in England, accused of being involved in a Papish plot, and died shortly after his release in 1682 at the age of 63.

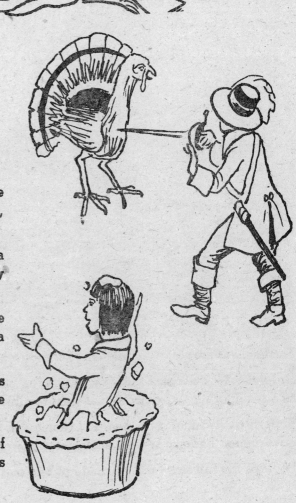

The PHILADELPHIA EXPERIMENT

One of the strangest and most terrifying experiments perhaps of all time took place during the last war.

In November 1943, an American convoy ship, moored in Philadelphia, suddenly disappeared before the astonished eyes of the official observers. Amazingly, at the same moment, it reappeared in the harbour of Norfolk, Virginia, nearly one thousand miles away. Immediately, it vanished from Norfolk to return to its original berth.

In 1942, a young scientist, Dr Morris K. Jessup, submitted a scientific thesis to the Naval Research Office based on one of Gilbert Einstein's theories, which would, by using a special combination of metals, create a powerful field of electricity, strong enough to displace any object.

The naval authorities were very interested. The idea being that whole convoys of ships crossing the Atlantic could beat the U-boat menace.

An experiment was duly made on the open sea in 1943.

The ship disappeared alright, but it kept reappearing and disappearing several times, it had become uncontrollable. Eventually, the terrifying spectacle came to an end, but it was found that most of the unfortunate crew had either been consumed by fire or had just vanished into wherever the ship had been in the disappearing episodes.

Most of the survivors became raving lunatics.

Einstein was asked for an explanation as to what had gone wrong but was unable to supply one.

Dr Jessup, the only man said to know the real story, was found dead in his car having committed suicide as a result of the experiment that went terribly wrong.

Reports of the incident appeared in some American papers but were immediately quashed by the US government under war-time emergency powers.

Perhaps the full story will be made public one day.

Moon Fire

Gervasius, a monk at Canterbury some 800 years ago, reported seeing a great burst of fire on the face of the moon.

He wondered if this was an omen of some great event on earth, but as time passed and nothing happened, scholars and others doubted his word and said he must have been seeing things.

But recently, Astonomer Jack B. Hartung of New York University, has vindicated the medieval monk by saying that what he saw was the impact of a huge meteor causing an explosion and fire on the moon's surface. The crash created the huge crater known as the Giordano Bruno.

? ? ? ? ? ? ? ?

What Would the Richest Person in the World Eat?

The answer, of course, is Caviar. The most expensive is Royal de luxe caviar which costs £224.50 for 500 g at Fortnum and Mason's in London.

The most expensive spice is wild ginseng from China. In 1977 this cost £10,454 per ounce in Hong Kong.

DIED OF OLD AGE – AT SEVEN!

Born 14th March, 1829, Charles Charlesworth of Staffordshire died seven years later — of old age!

From the very day he was born, he began to age rapidly and by the age of four, he was a fully developed man with a beard. At five his beard was white and his face lined and wizened, his hands gnarled and knotted, he needed a stick to hobble around.

By the age of six he was bent and shaking like an old man in his seventies, at seven he died of a heart attack.

Charles Charlesworth's body had crammed a life span of three score years and ten into just seven.

Can a Flower Predict the Weather?

The anwser is yes. The flowers of the plant called the scarlet pimpernel will give you a weather forecast. When the flowers close up, this is a good indication that rain or cloudy weather is coming. However, when the petals are open, the day should be fair and sunny. The nickname of this plant is "the poor man's weather glass".

Birthdays

Do you know why we blow out the candles on our birthday cake? It is a way of testing a child's strength. In olden times children played games and held competitions to see how strong they were becoming. We continue the custom of testing strength by trying to blow out all the candles on the cake with one big breath.

Each one of us shares our birthday with at least 10,000,000 other people. For some, it might be their first birthday, for others it could be their hundredth!

ATTILA THE HUN (died 453 AD)

LEADER OF THE BARBARIAN HORDES THAT OVER-RAN THE WESTERN CIVILISATION OF THE AGE AND KNOWN AS "THE SCOURGE OF GOD"—WAS A DWARF

FLY FISHER

THE APTLY NAMED ARCHER FISH OF INDIA, CATCHES FLIES BY SQUIRTING A DROP OF WATER FROM A GROOVE IN ITS MOUTH. THEY HAVE AN ACCURATE RANGE OF ABOUT 5 ft.

THE LARGEST SINGLE CHUNK OF GOLD EVER MINED WAS 4 ft. 9 ins. LONG, 3 ft. 2 ins. WIDE AND 4 ins. THICK AND WEIGHED 640 lbs. IT WAS DUG OUT IN NEW SOUTH WALES, AUSTRALIA, IN 1872. IT WAS VALUED THEN AT £29,600.

THE VALUABLE FUR KNOWN AS NUTRIA COMES FROM THE GIANT COYPU RAT. A NATIVE OF SOUTH AMERICA.

189

The Fear of Cold

American millionaire John Gottlieb Wendel, always wore boots or shoes with rubber soles at least an inch thick. He believed that germs of colds and other diseases entered the human body through soles of the feet.

But Mr Norris Peel, an old Yorkshireman, reckoned he remained free from colds by cutting the feet off his socks and taping the remainder to his legs, this way his feet could breathe and so he would never suffer from colds, flu, asthma or bronchitis.

The Swedish scholar, Professor Samuel Oedman, was so terrified of catching cold that he took to his bed — for the last 23 years of his life.

One winter day in 1829 an old farmer came to see him. Unfortunately he had snow on his clothes and Oedman promptly died of fright at the sight of it.

Howard Hughes, another eccentric American millionaire, had an obsession about germs. Members of his staff had to handle everything he might possibly touch with paper tissues.

Ferdinand II, Grand Duke of Tuscany in the 17th century, was a notorious health fanatic. If he felt the slightest hint of a cold coming on he paced up and down his room with a thermometer at each end which he watched for the slightest change in temperature. He carried several skull caps of varying thickness which he replaced one with the other when this happened.

Sleepy Tales

Very queer things can happen when you go sleepwalking as Belgian Leopold Foissart can testify. On holiday in Paris he walked in his sleep through the hotel and, while still asleep, put crosses again three horses in the newspaper he found. The following day he backed the horses he had picked — and won £6,400.

Before she went to bed, Mrs Hetty Lowe-Smythe put her valuable necklace carefully on her dressing table. Next morning it had vanished. The disappearance remained a mystery until two months later when she walked in her sleep and next morning awoke to find she was wearing it. Where it had been for two months she had no idea, that is when she was awake.

Another man Donald Messiter, of Paddington, London, didn't walk in his sleep but dreamed that his wife, Hilda, had got up in the middle of the night and dusted everything in the house.

Donald studied the horses in the morning paper and two stood out to him, Up and At It and Hilda's Hurricane. When he told his wife about his coincidence dream, she just laughed. But Donald put £5 on the horses.

Both won and turned the £5 into £211, enough for a holiday in Norway.

HOLY RATS

In the village of Deshnoke in India live thousands upon thousands of rats, in fact, it is a paradise for them — the villagers worship them! They believe that one of them is a reincarnation of the Hindu goddess Shri Karni Mata and the other rats are the ancestors of villagers and their friends.

Each day, the villagers go devoutly to the silver-ornamented temple to pray for the rodents and bring food and water and gifts of money, some £2,000 a year.

The people of Deshnoke say that when the goddess died over 400 years ago, she promised that she would return as a rat and if the people fed and respected them there would never be a plague of rats on the village's crops. The head priest says that the promise is being fulfilled and the village has never had such a plague. He also says "To us, the rats are our loved ones, that is why we feed and worship them, they are proof that our life will go on. They are proof that the miracles of Shri Karni Mata are continuing today".

The villagers reason that as the goddess chose to come back as a rat, they have to protect the rats and if anybody should accidentally hurt one, they are fined in silver or gold.

Animal Instincts

Elsewhere in this book, the destruction of the capital of Martinique, with the loss of 30,000 people when the volcano erupted, has a prelude.

They could have been saved if they had heeded the biggest animal warning ever recorded.

One calm and peaceful day, all the island's animals, both wild and domestic, suddenly went crazy. Hundreds of animals came from their homes — tearing through the streets, cats side by side with rats and all other kinds of creatures.

Across the country they rushed, headlong towards the beaches. They plunged straight into the sea and many were drowned. The island's human population were a little alarmed by this but the scientists at the island's observatory checked their seismograph, which picks up every shudder of the earth's crust, however slight, and assured them that there was no sign of an impending eruption and sent the islanders home.

Three days later the volcano blew its top.

BACK FROM THE GRAVE!

British General James L'Amy was absent from Jamaica for a few days and in his absence his fiancée was pronounced dead from the dreaded Yellow Fever. She was buried in the family mausoleum.

On his return the distraught general insisted that he see his beloved's face for the last time. As he did he saw a flicker of life. After a few sips of brandy she revived — and survived as his wife for another 41 years!

The Long, Long Wait . . .

Cabby Martin Holloway settled himself as comfortably as he could in the driver's seat of his cab. He had driven Lord Draggs, a noted yachtsman of his day, to the West Pier in Brighton on the afternoon of September 20th, 1887. His fare had asked him to wait whilst he took his new yacht for a trial run. "I expect to be back later this afternoon, so you can drive me home when I return," he said.

The cabby waited all afternoon but there was no sign of his Lordship. He went home and returned bright and early the next morning to resume the wait for the return of Lord Draggs.

Days stretched into weeks, weeks into months and still Martin Holloway waited, turning down people who wanted to hire him.

Finally, on 12th May, 1889, after a wait of 599 days, the patient cabby spotted his fare disembarking from his yacht. Lord Draggs explained that he had had every intention of returning the same afternoon, but once aboard he had decided to take an around the world trip.

Holloway pulled forth a sheet of paper with all his waiting time meticulously entered on it as required by police regulations. It came to a staggering £989 15s 6d. The only sign of surprise shown by his Lordship was a slight raising of the eyebrows, but he settled the bill, got into the cab and said, "Home, Martin!"

When the cab pulled into the driveway of Lord Dragg's manor, he alighted to find Holloway standing there with palm outstretched. "That'll be two bob for the trip, Sir," he said. His Lordship paid up.

Beauty Mystery

Slovakian Countess Zofia Bosniakova looks as beautiful today as she did when she was living nearly three and a half centuries ago, although her body was never embalmed.

Workmen were amazed when, during renovations to the crypt at Strecno Castle in 1689, they had a curious peep into her coffin. The Countess's body looked flawless even though she had been dead for 45 years and had suffered the heartbreak of two broken marriages.

Today she rests in a Chapel dedicated to her in Teplic, Czechoslavakia. She is dressed in a robe embroidered by herself. Although several dresses she has worn over the centuries have rotted away, her beauty has never faded.

How she remains as beautiful as when she died aged 35, is a complete mystery to scientists and a source of wonderment to the many pilgrims who visit the Lady of Strecno

Where Would You Find Squeeze-Belly Alley?

Squeeze-belly Alley is to be found in Port Isaac in Cornwall and is the world's narrowest street. At its narrowest point it is only $19\frac{5}{16}''$ (49 cm) wide.

The BIGGEST WASTREL

Prince of Galantha, Count of Edelstetten and hereditary Lord of Forchtenstein (1786–1866) Pál Antal Esterházy, was one of the richest men in Europe. His personal estate included 21 castles, 60 boroughs, 621 villages, 100,000 acres of land and 100,000 peasants.

To show his absolute disregard for value, he lined his coat with a priceless painting by Titian and when his racehorse won the 1819 Derby, he ordered it to be shot.

He squandered a fortune of about £5,000,000, a vast amount for those days. He is regarded as one of the biggest wastrels of the century.

Trunk Calls

Eccentric American millionaire William Randolph Hearst, was so fond of telephones that he had them fitted all over his house — and even in the gardens. Many were concealed in tree trunks.

WEREWOLF

1564 saw the start of a reign of terror that claimed over 200 men, women and children before the monster, one Peter Stubbe, was captured, tortured and executed in 1589.

He began with two or three killings, believed to be in revenge for some insult, real or imagined.

At first the gruesome mutilation of the victims and partly eaten remains led the authorities of nearby Cologne to believe that it must be wolves that were carrying out the attacks. But as the number of deaths grew a certain pattern formed. The limbs were scattered about, the skulls were split open and the brains removed, the heart and entrails were torn out and laid aside The word went around that struck terror into the hearts of everyone — WEREWOLF

The mayor of Cologne organised volunteers to hide in the surrounding countryside. Suspicion centred on Stubbe, a wealthy local tradesman, many of the victims were known to him and some were business rivals of his.

Subsequently, it was alleged, Stubbe had been seen walking in the woods, where he dropped on all fours like an animal, howled and ran off at great speed

Under torture he was said to have shown how he could sprout hair on his body, turn his nails into claws and change the shape of his teeth. On his own admission he had killed and eaten more than 200 people. It is the only documented case of a man admitting to being a werewolf.

Thousands of people crowded the square of the small town of Bedburg, to watch the execution on October 31, 1589, of the man who could turn himself into a wolf.

Did you know . . .

. . . that every tenth egg laid is larger than the nine eggs which were laid before it?

Did you know . . .

. . . that there is less sugar in 1 kg of strawberries than in the equivalent weight of lemons?

Did you know . . .

. . . a litre of vinegar weighs more in winter than it does in summer?

Did you know . . .

. . . that an egg weighs more when first laid than when it is about to hatch?

Did you know . . .

. . . you could make seven bars of soap from the fat in your body?

When Is a 3-Minute Egg Not a 3-Minute Egg?

If you cooked an egg at the top of a high mountain — at least 5,000 feet above sea level, your 3-minute egg would take 4 minutes to cook.

This is because the air is less dense and exerts less pressure which enables the water to boil sooner and at a lower temperature so the egg must be cooked for one minute longer.

Obstinate Oranges

If you pick an orange too early, it will remain unripe. Oranges refuse to ripen unless on the tree, unlike most fruit which will ripen when picked.

Who Grows the Most Pineapples?

Over a third of the world's supply are grown on the small islands of Hawaii.

FOOD FOR THOUGHT

If you were getting married many years ago in Europe, you would probably have been given an onion as a present! A long time ago, onions were considered very valuable.

If you died 5,000 years ago in Egypt, you would have had the inside of your tomb decorated with paintings of onions. The Egyptians also used an onion, as we would use the Bible, to swear an oath.

The onion takes its name from the latin word "unio" which means "large pearl".

Most people would say that garlic is a relative of the onion. It is, in fact, a relative of the lily family!

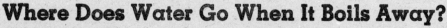

When Is a Pilchard Not a Pilchard?

When it's packed in a tin, it's a sardine!

A sardine is purely a name only — you are really eating herring or pilchards, which when packed in tins, are called sardines.

Where Did Spaghetti Originate?

Well, it wasn't from Italy! Spaghetti originally came from China some 800 years ago. Chinese spaghetti is called Lo Mein and is used in the best Chinese cookery. Why don't you try some?

Where Does Water Go When It Boils Away?

When the water is boiled, it doesn't disappear, it changes its structure. The water changes into steam which collects and appears as clouds in the sky. When these clouds meet cool air, the water condenses into droplets and falls as rain. The rain forms streams and rivers which flow into reservoirs after which it is purified and flows into our taps, to start the cycle again.

FOOD FOR THOUGHT

An Apple a Day Keeps the Doctor Away

There is no evidence to substantiate this saying. Apples do not contain any magical ingredients. However, they do give us much of the potassium we need. This, combined with other minerals, helps to keep us healthy.

Did you know that there are nearly 10,000 different varieties of apples?

Why Sandwich?

We have all eaten sandwiches at sometime or other, but they were unknown until the eighteenth century. The Fourth Earl of Sandwich unwittingly gave his name to this convenient snack.

He was a compulsive gambler and could not even bring himself to leave a card game to eat proper meals. Instead, he instructed his staff to put pieces of cooked meat between two slices of bread and was thus able to eat with one hand and continue playing cards with the other, and so the sandwich was invented.

The popularity of this simple idea soon grew. Lots of people began to enjoy sandwiches because they could be easily prepared and eaten.

What Is Your Least Favourite Job At Home?

I bet it's doing the washing-up.

Things were much better hundreds of years ago when the first plates were made of bread so that they could actually be eaten. They were made from crusts baked hard not very tasty but it beats washing up!

The Tomato — Fruit or Vegetable?

Strangely enough, the tomato is classed as a fruit by botanists because it contains seeds. It is regarded as a berry, like the raspberry or strawberry.

Some other foods we use as vegetables are regarded as fruits — runner beans and cucumbers for example.

199

Misleading Names

RICE PAPER — is not made from rice. It is made from wood pulp.

BUTTERMILK — contains no butter at all.

SODA WATER — contains no soda.

BELGIAN HARE — is not a hare, it's a rabbit.

STILTON CHEESE — originally came from Leicestershire, a place called the Vale of Belvoir.

BOMBAY DUCK — is not, as you would think made from duck, but made from fish and curry. It doesn't contain any duck at all!

Food From Heaven?

In the old Testament, we read about "manna" which God provided for the Israelites in the wilderness.

There are various explanations for this, one being that it is "honeydew" secreted by some kinds of insect, another theory is that it is an edible lichen "lecanora esculenta".

Why Should You Only Eat Oysters When There Is An "R" In the Month?

The reason for this superstition is that in the months of May, June, July and August, the oysters will be tough as they are laying eggs during these months.

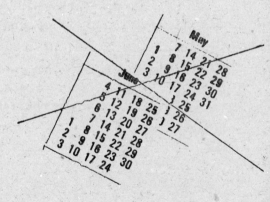

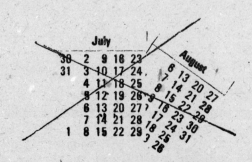

American Assets

The mangrove, a tropical evergreen tree, is one of the few trees that will grow in salt water. It is found in swampy areas and riverbanks, in some countries such as America, it is used to help reclaim land.

America has contributed many things to the world including:

TAPIOCA — made from the starchy roots of a tropical plant called cassava.

TOBACCO — another American tropical plant, relative of the nightshade family. The large sticky leaves are dried and cured. It is then rolled for cigars, shredded for cigarettes and powdered for snuff.

TOMATO — introduced to Europe in 16th century from the United States.

TURKEY — the Turkey comes from Mexico. Also introduced to Europe during 16th century.

If you went into a restaurant a few hundred years ago, you may be a little confused on reading the menu — tea would be written as "tay" and an apple would appear as "a napple". You wouldn't however, find any tomatoes on the menu — they would be out in the garden, as at that time, they were considered poisonous and used as unusual garden plants!

You would, without doubt, find broad beans on the menu — they are the oldest vegetable known.

Productive Palms

In the islands of the Seychelles, the inhabitants grow palms which produce huge, double coconuts which can weigh up to 18 kgs!

Delicious Decoration

When the first potato was introduced here in the 1570s from South America, the Europeans wouldn't eat it! They thought it was poisonous and they grew it purely for its flowers which the women wore in their hair and the men wore in their lapels. This went on for some two hundred years until someone discovered that potatoes were edible.

FOOD FOR THOUGHT

Why Is Champagne Shaken?

When champagne is very young (three or four months old), every bottle is shaken carefully to ensure that all the sediment is at the "cork end" which makes the champagne easier to clear.

How Old Is the Best Port?

Vintage port takes 40 years to reach its best. It is then said to be "mature".

☆ ☆ ☆ ☆ ☆ ☆ ☆

Which Soft Drink Is Sold In Over 147 Different Countries?

Coca Cola — the most popular soft drink of all time!

How much do we drink?

250,000,000 bottles are consumed every day around the world.

Who knows the secret formula?

So few people know how to make Coca Cola that it is one of the best "trade secrets" ever kept.

How Many Animals Can You Name Which Give Us Milk?

Not only the cow and the goat are used for milk and cheese making, in some parts of the world, farmers milk reindeer, llamas and yaks!

THE MAN WHO STOLE THE ROYAL CROWN

In 1671 a man, disguised as one of the clergy, stole the Crown of England from the Tower of London, was tracked down by royal agents and captured in a public house called the Crown and Cushion!

He was Colonel Thomas Blood, an Irish adventurer with estates in Ireland. He and three accomplices went to the Tower intending to steal the Crown Jewels.

After almost killing the elderly Keeper of the Jewels he escaped with the crown under his cloak and an accomplice took the Orb.

Blood was seized and taken back to the tower — this time in chains. King Charles II visited him in his cell and talked with him for quite a while. Later the King pardoned Blood, restored his estates in Ireland and granted him £500 a year.

The reason for this Royal magnanimity has never been quite clear but it is thought that possibly the monarch feared the revenge of the hundreds of followers on oath to avenge Blood's death. Until his death in 1680 Blood had great influence at court.

To commemorate the capture a yew tree was planted at the inn at Minley in Hampshire, and has been trimmed ever since in the shape of a crown resting on the cushion.

★ ★ ★ ★ ★ ★ ★

300 MILE CRAWL

The father and two sons crawled down the dusty road to Hardwar, India, on their hands and knees. They were doing it as the man's thanksgiving for the recovery of his son from typhus having vowed to crawl the 300 miles from Manosa to Hardwar, taking his two sons with him.

After one week of the journey, his younger son, still weak from his illness, collapsed and died by the roadside. Doctors warned him of the futility of carrying on but to no avail, the man's religion forbade him to break his vow.

On they crawled, weary and bleeding until, just ten miles from their destination, the second son died.

Still the father carried on and completed his journey in 68 days — every bit of the way on all fours.

Returning home three weeks later the cart in which he was travelling overturned and killed the father who could not break his vow — by a quirk of fate just two yards from the road on which his sons had died.

LAST LAUGHS

FOUND ON GRAVESTONES THROUGHOUT THE WORLD

Ellen Shannon
aged 26
Who was fatally burned
March 21 1870
by the explosion of a lamp
filled with
R.E. Danforth's Non-Explosive
Burning Fluid

Girard, Penn. U.S.A.

Here lies Ann Mann
She lived an Old Maid
And died an Old Mann

England

WAGNER
He argued with
the wrong man's
brother

Epitaph of the man who
gunned down Bat Master-
son's brother. Boot Hill,
Dodge City, Kansas, U.S.A.

ARTHUR HAINE
ATHEIST
HAINE - HAINT

Vancouver, Canada.

An auctioneer named
KNIGHT
GOOD KNIGHT
GOING
GOING
GONE
1868

Greenwood, England

Shoot-em-up
JAKE
Run for sherrif 1872
Run from sherrif 1876
Buried 1876

Boot Hill, Dodge City, U.S.A

Here lies an atheist
all dressed up
and no place to go

Maryland U.S.A.

Here lies the body of
Solomon Peas
Under the daisies and
under the trees
Peas is not here —
only the pod
Peas shelled out
went home to God.

Wetumpha, Al. U.S.A.

Here lies the body of John Mound
Lost at Sea and never found.

Ireland

A Wells Fargo agent
called Les Moore

Here lies Lester
Moore
Four slugs from
a .44
No Les, no Moore

Boot Hill,
Dodge City